The War in South Africa
Its Cause and Conduct

By Arthur Conan Doyle

TABLE OF CONTENTS

PREFACE

For some reason, which may be either arrogance or apathy, the British are very slow to state their case to the world. At present the reasons for our actions and the methods which we have used are set forth in many Blue-books, tracts, and leaflets, but have never, so far as I know, been collected into one small volume. In view of the persistent slanders to which our politicians and our soldiers have been equally exposed, it becomes a duty which we owe to our national honour to lay the facts before the world. I wish someone more competent, and with some official authority, had undertaken the task, which I have tried to do as best I might from an independent standpoint.

There was never a war in history in which the right was absolutely on one side, or in which no incidents of the campaign were open to criticism. I do not pretend that it was so here. But I do not think that any unprejudiced man can read the facts without acknowledging that the British Government has done its best to avoid war, and the British Army to wage it with humanity.

To my publisher and to myself this work has been its own reward. In this way we hope to put the price within the reach of all, and yet leave a profit for the vendor. Our further ambition is, however, to translate it into all European tongues, and to send a free copy to every deputy and every newspaper on the Continent and in America. For this work money will be needed—a considerable sum. We propose to make an appeal to the public for these funds. Any sums which are sent to me or to my publisher will be devoted to this work. There cannot be too much, for the more we get the more we shall do.

I may add that I have not burdened my pages with continual references. My quotations are reliable and can always, if necessary, be substantiated.

A. CONAN DOYLE, UNDERSHAW, HINDHEAD, January, 1902.

I. THE BOER PEOPLE

It is impossible to appreciate the South African problem and the causes which have led up to the present war between the British Empire and the Boer republics without some knowledge, however superficial, of the past history of South Africa. To tell the tale one must go back to the beginning, for there has been complete continuity of history in South Africa, and every stage has depended upon that which has preceded it. No one can know or appreciate the Boer who does not know his past, for he is what his past has made him.

It was about the time when Oliver Cromwell was at his zenith—in 1652, to be pedantically accurate—that the Dutch made their first lodgment at the Cape of Good Hope. The Portuguese had been there before them, but, repelled by the evil weather, and lured forward by rumours of gold, they had passed the true seat of empire, and had voyaged farther, to settle along the eastern coast. But the Dutchmen at the Cape prospered and grew stronger in that robust climate. They did not penetrate far inland, for they were few in number, and all they wanted was to be found close at hand. But they built themselves houses, and they supplied the Dutch East India Company with food and water, gradually budding off little townlets, Wynberg, Stellenbosch, and pushing their settlements up the long slopes which lead to that great central plateau which extends for 1,500 miles from the edge of the Karoo to the Valley of the Zambesi.

For a hundred more years the history of the colony was a record of the gradual spreading of the Africanders over the huge expanse of veldt which lay to the north of them. Cattle-raising became an industry, but in a country where six acres can hardly support a sheep, large farms are necessary for even small herds. Six thousand acres was the usual size, and 5£. a year the rent payable to Government. The diseases which follow the white man had in Africa, as in America and Australia, been fatal to the natives, and an epidemic of smallpox cleared the country for the new-comers. Farther and farther north they pushed, founding little towns here and there, such as Graaf-Reinet and Swellendam, where a Dutch Reformed Church and a store for the sale of the bare necessaries of life formed a nucleus for a few scattered dwellings. Already the settlers were showing that independence of control and that detachment from Europe which has been their most prominent characteristic. Even the mild sway of the Dutch Company had caused them to revolt. The local rising, however, was hardly noticed in the universal cataclysm which followed the French Revolution. After twenty years, during which the world was shaken by the Titanic struggle in the final counting up of the game and paying of the stakes, the Cape Colony was added in 1814 to the British Empire.

In all the vast collection of British States there is probably not one the title-deeds to which are more incontestable than to this. Britain had it by two rights, the right of conquest and the right of purchase. In 1806 troops landed, defeated the local forces, and took possession of Cape Town. In 1814 Britain paid the large sum of six million pounds to the Stadtholder for the transference of this and some South American land. It was a bargain which was probably made rapidly and carelessly in that general redistribution which was going on. As a house of call upon the way to India the place was seen to be of value, but the country itself was looked upon as unprofitable and desert. What would Castlereagh or Liverpool have thought could they have seen the items which they were buying for six million pounds? The inventory would have been a mixed one of good and of evil: nine fierce Kaffir wars, the greatest diamond mines in the world, the wealthiest gold mines, two costly and humiliating campaigns with men whom we respected even when we fought with them, and now at last, we hope, a South Africa of peace and prosperity, with equal rights and equal duties for all men.

The title-deeds to the estate are, as I have said, good ones, but there is one singular and ominous flaw in their provisions. The ocean has marked three boundaries to it, but the fourth is undefined. There is no word of the 'hinterland,' for neither the term nor the idea had then been thought of. Had Great Britain bought those vast regions which extended beyond the settlements? Or were the discontented Dutch at liberty to pass onwards and found fresh nations to bar the path of the Anglo-Celtic colonists? In that question lay the germ of all the trouble to come. An American would realise the point at issue if he could conceive that after the founding of the United States the Dutch inhabitants of the State of New York had trekked to the westward and established fresh communities under a new flag. Then, when the American population overtook these western States, they would be face to face with the problem which this country has had to solve. If they found these new States fiercely anti-American and extremely unprogressive, they would experience that aggravation of their difficulties with which British statesmen have had to deal.

At the time of their transference to the British flag the colonists—Dutch, French, and German—numbered some thirty thousand. They were slaveholders, and the slaves were about as numerous as themselves. The prospect of complete amalgamation between the British and the original settlers would have seemed to be a good one, since they were of much the same stock, and their creeds could only be distinguished by their varying degrees of bigotry and intolerance. Five thousand British emigrants were landed in 1820, settling on the Eastern borders of the colony, and from that time onwards there was a slow but steady influx of English-speaking colonists. The Government had the historical faults and the historical virtues of British rule. It was mild, clean, honest, tactless, and inconsistent. On the whole, it might have done very well had it been content to leave things as it found them. But to change the habits of the most conservative of Teutonic races was a dangerous venture, and one which has led to a long series of complications, making up the troubled history of South Africa.

The Imperial Government has always taken an honourable and philanthropic view of the rights of the native and the claim which he has to the protection of the law. We hold, and rightly, that British justice, if not blind, should at least be colour-blind. The view is irreproachable in theory and incontestable in argument, but it is apt to be irritating when urged by a Boston moralist or a London philanthropist upon men whose whole society has been built upon the assumption that the black is the inferior race. Such a people like to find the higher morality for themselves, not to have it imposed upon them by those who live under entirely different conditions.

The British Government in South Africa has always played the unpopular part of the friend and protector of the native servants. It was upon this very point that the first friction appeared between the old settlers and the new administration. A rising with bloodshed followed the arrest of a Dutch farmer who had maltreated his slave. It was suppressed, and five of the participants were hanged. This punishment was unduly severe and exceedingly injudicious. A brave race can forget the victims of the field of battle, but never those of the scaffold. The making of political martyrs is the last insanity of statesmanship. However, the thing was done, and it is typical of the enduring resentment which was left behind that when, after the Jameson Raid, it seemed that the leaders of that ill-fated venture might be hanged, the beam was actually brought from a farmhouse at Cookhouse Drift to Pretoria, that the Englishmen might die as the Dutchmen had died in 1816. Slagter's Nek marked the dividing of the ways between the British Government and the Africanders.

And the separation soon became more marked. With vicarious generosity, the English Government gave very lenient terms to the Kaffir tribes who in 1834 had raided the border farmers. And then, finally, in this same year there came the emancipation of the slaves throughout the British Empire, which fanned all smouldering discontents into an active flame.

It must be confessed that on this occasion the British philanthropist was willing to pay for what he thought was right. It was a noble national action, and one the morality of which was in advance of its time, that the British Parliament should vote the enormous sum of twenty million pounds to pay compensation to the slaveholders, and so to remove an evil with which the mother country had no immediate connection. It was as well that the thing should have been done when it was, for had we waited till the colonies affected had governments of their own it could never have been done by constitutional methods. With many a grumble the good British householder drew his purse from his fob, and paid for what he thought to be right. If any special grace attends the virtuous action which brings nothing but tribulation in this world, then we may hope for it over this emancipation. We spent our money, we ruined our West Indian colonies, and we started a disaffection in South Africa, the end of which we have not seen.

But the details of the measure were less honourable than the principle. It was carried out suddenly, so that the country had no time to adjust itself to the new conditions. Three million pounds were ear-marked for South Africa, which gives a price per slave of from 60£. to 70£., a sum considerably below the current local rates. Finally, the compensation was made payable in London, so that the farmers sold their claims at reduced prices to middlemen. Indignation meetings were held in every little townlet and cattle-camp on the Karoo. The old Dutch spirit was up—the spirit of the men who cut the dykes. Rebellion was useless. But a vast untenanted land stretched to the north of them.

The nomad life was congenial to them, and in their huge ox-drawn wagons—like those bullock-carts in which some of their old kinsmen came to Gaul—they had vehicles and homes and forts all in one. One by one they were loaded up, the huge teams were inspanned, the women were seated inside, the men with their long-barrelled guns walked alongside, and the great exodus was begun. Their herds and flocks accompanied the migration, and the children helped to round them in and drive them. One tattered little boy of ten cracked his sjambok whip behind the bullocks. He was a small item in that singular crowd, but he was of interest to us, for his name was Paul Stephanus Kruger.

It was a strange exodus, only comparable in modern times to the sallying forth of the Mormons from Nauvoo upon their search for the promised land of Utah. The country was known and sparsely settled as far north as the Orange River, but beyond there was a great region which had never been penetrated save by some daring hunter or adventurous pioneer. It chanced—if there be indeed such an element as chance in the graver affairs of man—that a Zulu conqueror had swept over this land and left it untenanted, save by the dwarf bushmen, the hideous aborigines, lowest of the human race. There were fine grazing and good soil for the emigrants. They travelled in small detached parties, but their total numbers were considerable, from six to ten thousand according to their historian, or nearly a quarter of the whole population of the colony. Some of the early bands perished miserably. A large number made a trysting-place at a high peak to the east of Bloemfontein, in what was lately the Orange Free State. One party of the emigrants was cut off by the formidable Matabeli, a branch of the great Zulu nation.

The final victory of the 'voortrekkers' cleared all the country between the Orange River and the Limpopo, the sites of what have been known as the Transvaal and the Orange Free State. In the meantime another body of the emigrants had descended into Natal, and had defeated Dingaan, the great Chief of the Zulus.

And now at the end of their great journey, after overcoming the difficulties of distance, of nature, and of savage enemies, the Boers saw at the end of their travels the very thing which they desired least—that which they had come so far to avoid—the flag of Great Britain. The Boers had occupied Natal from within, but England had previously done the same by sea, and a small colony of Englishmen had settled at Port Natal, now known as Durban. The home Government, however, had acted in a vacillating way, and it was only the conquest of Natal by the Boers which caused them to claim it as a British colony. At the same time they asserted the unwelcome doctrine that a British subject could not at will throw off his allegiance, and that, go where they might, the wandering farmers were still only the pioneers of British colonies. To emphasise the fact three companies of soldiers were sent in 1842 to what is now Durban—the usual Corporal's guard with which Great Britain starts a new empire. This handful of men was waylaid by the Boers and cut up, as their successors have been so often since. The survivors, however, fortified themselves, and held a defensive position—as also their successors have done so many times since—until reinforcements arrived and the farmers dispersed. Natal from this time onward became a British colony, and the majority of the Boers trekked north and east with bitter hearts to tell their wrongs to their brethren of the Orange Free State and of the Transvaal.

Had they any wrongs to tell? It is difficult to reach that height of philosophic detachment which enables the historian to deal absolutely impartially where his own country is a party to the quarrel. But at least we may allow that there is a case for our adversary. Our annexation of Natal had been by no means definite, and it was they and not we who first broke that bloodthirsty Zulu power which threw its shadow across the country. It was hard after such trials and such exploits to turn their back upon the fertile land which they had conquered, and to return to the bare pastures of the upland veldt. They carried out of Natal a heavy sense of injury, which has helped to poison our relations with them ever since. It was, in a way, a momentous episode, this little skirmish of soldiers and emigrants, for it was the heading off of the Boer from the sea and the confinement of his ambition to the land. Had it gone the other way, a new and possibly formidable flag would have been added to the maritime nations.

The emigrants who had settled in the huge tract of country between the Orange River in the south and the Limpopo in the north had been recruited by new-comers from the Cape Colony until they numbered some fifteen thousand souls. This population was scattered over a space as large as Germany, and larger than Pennsylvania, New York, and New England. Their form of government was individualistic and democratic to the last degree compatible with any sort of cohesion. Their wars with the Kaffirs and their fear and dislike of the British Government appear to have been the only ties which held them together. They divided and subdivided within their own borders, like a germinating egg. The Transvaal was full of lusty little high-mettled communities, who quarrelled among themselves as fiercely as they had done with the authorities at the Cape. Lydenburg, Zoutpansberg, and Potchefstroom were on the point of turning their rifles against each other. In the south, between the Orange River and the Vaal, there was no form of government at all, but a welter of Dutch farmers, Basutos, Hottentots, and half-breeds living in a chronic state of turbulence, recognising neither the British authority to the south of them nor the Transvaal republics to the north. The chaos became at last unendurable, and in 1848 a garrison was placed in Bloemfontein and the district incorporated in the British Empire. The emigrants made a futile resistance at Boomplaats, and after a single defeat allowed themselves to be drawn into the settled order of civilised rule.

At this period the Transvaal, where most of the Boers had settled, desired a formal acknowledgment of their independence, which the British authorities determined once and for all to give them. The great barren country, which produced little save marksmen, had no attractions for a Colonial Office which was bent upon the limitation of its liabilities. A Convention was concluded between the two parties, known as the Sand River Convention, which is one of the fixed points in South African history. By it the British Government guaranteed to the Boer farmers the right to manage their own affairs, and to govern themselves by their own laws without any interference upon the part of the British. It stipulated that there should be no slavery, and with that single reservation washed its hands finally, as it imagined, of the whole question. So the Transvaal Republic came formally into existence.

In the very year after the Sand River Convention, a second republic, the Orange Free State, was created by the deliberate withdrawal of Great Britain from the territory which she had for eight years occupied. The Eastern Question was already becoming acute, and the cloud of a great war was drifting up, visible to all men. British statesmen felt that their commitments were very heavy in every part of the world, and the South African annexations had always been a doubtful value and an undoubted trouble. Against the will of a large part of the inhabitants, whether a majority or not it is impossible to say, we withdrew our troops as amicably as the Romans withdrew from Britain, and the new republic was left with absolute and unfettered independence. On a petition being presented against the withdrawal, the Home Government actually voted 48,000£ to compensate those who had suffered from the change. Whatever historical grievance the Transvaal may have against Great Britain, we can at least, save perhaps in one matter, claim to have a very clear conscience concerning our dealings with the Orange Free State. Thus in 1852 and in 1854 were born those sturdy States who have been able for a time to hold at bay the united forces of the Empire.

In the meantime Cape Colony, in spite of these secessions, had prospered exceedingly, and her population—British, German, and Dutch—had grown by 1870 to over two hundred thousand souls, the Dutch still slightly predominating. According to the liberal colonial policy of Great Britain, the time had come to cut the cord and let the young nation conduct its own affairs. In 1872 complete self-government was given to it, the Governor, as the representative of the Queen, retaining a nominal unexercised veto upon legislation. According to this system the Dutch majority of the colony could, and did, put their own representatives into power and run the government upon Dutch lines. Already Dutch law had been restored, and Dutch put on the same footing as English as the official language of the country. The extreme liberality of such measures, and the uncompromising way in which they have been carried out, however distasteful the legislation might seem to English ideas, are among the chief reasons which made the illiberal treatment of British settlers in the Transvaal so keenly resented at the Cape. A Dutch Government was ruling the British in a British colony, at a moment when the Boers would not give an Englishman a vote upon a municipal council in a city which he had built himself.

For twenty-five years after the Sand River Convention the burghers of the Transvaal Republic had pursued a strenuous and violent existence, fighting incessantly with the natives and sometimes with each other, with an occasional fling at the little Dutch republic to the south. Disorganisation ensued. The burghers would not pay taxes and the treasury was empty. One fierce Kaffir tribe threatened them from the north, and the Zulus on the east. It is an exaggeration to pretend that British intervention saved the Boers, for no one can read their military history without seeing that they were a match for Zulus and Sekukuni combined. But certainly a formidable invasion was pending, and the scattered farmhouses were as open to the Kaffirs as our farmers' homesteads were in the American colonies when the Indians were on the war-path. Sir Theophilus Shepstone, the British Commissioner, after an inquiry of three months, solved all questions by the formal annexation of the country. The fact that he took possession of it with a force of some twenty-five men showed the honesty of his belief that no armed resistance was to be feared. This, then, in 1877, was a complete reversal of the Sand River Convention and the opening of a new chapter in the history of South Africa.

There did not appear to be any strong feeling at the time against the annexation. The people were depressed with their troubles and weary of contention. Burgers, the President, put in a formal protest, and took up his abode in Cape Colony, where he had a pension from the British Government. A memorial against the measure received the signatures of a majority of the Boer inhabitants, but there was a fair minority who took the other view. Kruger himself accepted a paid office under Government. There was every sign that the people, if judiciously handled, would settle down under the British flag.

But the Empire has always had poor luck in South Africa, and never worse than on that occasion. Through no bad faith, but simply through preoccupation and delay, the promises made were not instantly fulfilled. If the Transvaalers had waited, they would have had their Volksraad and all that they wanted. But the British Government had some other local matters to set right, the rooting out of Sekukuni and the breaking of the Zulus, before they would fulfil their pledges. The delay was keenly resented. And we were unfortunate in our choice of Governor. The burghers are a homely folk, and they like an occasional cup of coffee with the anxious man who tries to rule them. The 300£. a year of coffee-money allowed by the Transvaal to its President is by no means a mere form. A wise administrator would fall into the social and democratic habits of the people. Sir Theophilus Shepstone did so. Sir Owen Lanyon did not. There was no Volksraad and no coffee, and the popular discontent grew rapidly. In three years the British had broken up the two savage hordes which had been threatening the land. The finances, too, had been restored. The reasons which had made so many burghers favour the annexation were weakened by the very power which had every interest in preserving them.

It cannot be too often pointed out that in this annexation, the starting- point of our troubles, Great Britain, however mistaken she may have been, had no possible selfish interest in view. There were no Rand mines in those days, nor was there anything in the country to tempt the most covetous. An empty treasury and two expensive native wars were the reversion which we took over. It was honestly considered that the country was in too distracted a state to govern itself, and had, by its weakness, become a scandal and a danger to its neighbours and to itself. There was nothing sordid in the British action, though it may have been premature and injudicious. There is some reason to think that if it had been delayed it would eventually have been done on the petition of the majority of the inhabitants.

In December 1880 the Boers rose. Every farmhouse sent out its riflemen, and the trysting-place was the outside of the nearest British fort. All through the country small detachments were surrounded and besieged by the farmers. Standerton, Pretoria, Potchefstroom, Lydenburg, Wakkerstroom, Rustenburg, and Marabastad were all invested and all held out until the end of the war. In the open country the troops were less fortunate. At Bronkhorst Spruit a small British force was taken by surprise and shot down without harm to their antagonists. The surgeon who treated them has left it on record that the average number of wounds was five per man. At Laing's Nek an inferior force of British endeavoured to rush a hill which was held by Boer riflemen. Half of the men were killed and wounded. Ingogo may be called a drawn battle, though the British loss was more heavy than that of the enemy. Finally came the defeat of Majuba Hill, where 400 infantry upon a mountain were defeated and driven off by a swarm of sharpshooters who advanced under the cover of boulders. Of all these actions there was not one which was more than a skirmish, and had they been followed by a final British victory they would now be hardly remembered. It is the fact that they were skirmishes which succeeded in their object which has given them an importance which is exaggerated.

The defeat at Majuba Hill was followed by the complete surrender of the Gladstonian Government, an act which was either the most pusillanimous or the most magnanimous in recent history. It is hard for the big man to draw away from the small before blows are struck, but when the big man has been knocked down three times it is harder still. An overwhelming British force was in the field, and the General declared that he held the enemy in the hollow of his hand. British military calculations have been falsified before now by these farmers, and it may be that the task of Wood and Roberts would have been harder than they imagined; but on paper, at least, it looked as if the enemy could be crushed without difficulty. So the public thought, and yet they consented to the upraised sword being stayed. With them, as apart from the politicians, the motive was undoubtedly a moral and Christian one. They considered that the annexation of the Transvaal had evidently been an injustice, that the farmers had a right to the freedom for which they fought, and that it was an unworthy thing for a great nation to continue an unjust war for the sake of a military revenge. Such was the motive of the British public when it acquiesced in the action of the Government. It was the height of idealism, and the result has not been such as to encourage its repetition.

An armistice was concluded on March 5, 1881, which led up to a peace on the 23rd of the same month. The Government, after yielding to force what it had repeatedly refused to friendly representations, made a clumsy compromise in their settlement. A policy of idealism and Christian morality should have been thorough if it were to be tried at all. It was obvious that if the annexation were unjust, then the Transvaal should have reverted to the condition in which it was before the annexation, as defined by the Sand River Convention. But the Government for some reason would not go so far as this. They niggled and quibbled and bargained until the State was left as a curious hybrid thing such as the world has never seen. It was a republic which was part of the system of a monarchy, dealt with by the Colonial Office, and included under the heading of 'Colonies' in the news columns of the 'Times.' It was autonomous, and yet subject to some vague suzerainty, the limits of which no one has ever been able to define. Altogether, in its provisions and in its omissions, the Convention of Pretoria appears to prove that our political affairs were as badly conducted as our military in this unfortunate year of 1881.

It was evident from the first that so illogical and contentious an agreement could not possibly prove to be a final settlement, and indeed the ink of the signatures was hardly dry before an agitation was on foot for its revision. The Boers considered, and with justice, that if they were to be left as undisputed victors in the war then they should have the full fruits of victory. On the other hand, the English-speaking colonies had their allegiance tested to the uttermost. The proud Anglo-Celtic stock is not accustomed to be humbled, and yet they found themselves through the action of the home Government converted into members of a beaten race. It was very well for the citizen of London to console his wounded pride by the thought that he had done a magnanimous action, but it was different with the British colonist of Durban or Cape Town who, by no act of his own, and without any voice in the settlement, found himself humiliated before his Dutch neighbour. An ugly feeling of resentment was left behind, which might perhaps have passed away had the Transvaal accepted the settlement in the spirit in which it was meant, but which grew more and more dangerous, as during eighteen years our people saw, or thought that they saw, that one concession led always to a fresh demand, and that the Dutch republics aimed not merely at equality, but at dominance in South Africa. Professor Bryce, a friendly critic, after a personal examination of the country and the question, has left it upon record that the Boers saw neither generosity nor humanity in our conduct, but only fear. An outspoken race, they conveyed their feelings to their neighbours. Can it be wondered at that South Africa has been in a ferment ever since, and that the British Africander has yearned with an intensity of feeling unknown in England for the hour of revenge?

The Government of the Transvaal after the war was left in the hands of a triumvirate, but after one year Kruger became President, an office which he continued to hold for eighteen years. His career as ruler vindicates the wisdom of that wise but unwritten provision of the American Constitution by which there is a limit to the tenure of this office. Continued rule for half a generation must turn a man into an autocrat. The old President has said himself, in his homely but shrewd way, that when one gets a good ox to lead the team it is a pity to change him. If a good ox, however, is left to choose his own direction without guidance, he may draw his wagon into trouble.

During three years the little State showed signs of a tumultuous activity. Considering that it was larger than France and that the population could not have been more than fifty thousand, one would have thought that they might have found room without any inconvenient crowding. But the burghers passed beyond their borders in every direction. The President cried aloud that he had been shut up in a kraal, and he proceeded to find ways out of it. A great trek was projected for the north, but fortunately it miscarried. To the east they raided Zululand, and succeeded, in defiance of the British settlement of that country, in tearing away one-third of it and adding it to the Transvaal. To the west, with no regard to the three-year-old treaty, they invaded Bechuanaland, and set up the two new republics of Goshen and Stellaland. So outrageous were these proceedings that Great Britain was forced to fit out in 1884 a new expedition under Sir Charles Warren for the purpose of turning these freebooters out of the country. It may be asked, why should these men be called freebooters if the founders of Rhodesia were pioneers? The answer is that the Transvaal was limited by treaty to certain boundaries which these men transgressed, while no pledges were broken when the British power expanded to the north. The upshot of these trespasses was the scene upon which every drama of South Africa rings down. Once more the purse was drawn from the pocket of the unhappy taxpayer, and a million or so was paid out to defray the expenses of the police force necessary to keep these treaty-breakers in order. Let this be borne in mind when we assess the moral and material damage done to the Transvaal by the Jameson Raid.

In 1884 a deputation from the Transvaal visited England, and at their solicitation the clumsy Treaty of Pretoria was altered into the still more clumsy Convention of London. The changes in the provisions were all in favour of the Boers, and a second successful war could hardly have given them more than Lord Derby handed them in time of peace. Their style was altered from the Transvaal to the South African Republic, a change which was ominously suggestive of expansion in the future. The control of Great Britain over their foreign policy was also relaxed, though a power of veto was retained. But the most important thing of all, and the fruitful cause of future trouble, lay in an omission. A suzerainty is a vague term, but in politics, as in theology, the more nebulous a thing is the more does it excite the imagination and the passions of men. This suzerainty was declared in the preamble of the first treaty, and no mention of it was made in the second. Was it thereby abrogated or was it not? The British contention is that only the articles were changed, and that the preamble continued to hold good for both treaties. They point out that not only the suzerainty, but also the independence, of the Transvaal is proclaimed in that preamble, and that if one lapses the other must do so also. On the other hand, the Boers point to the fact that there is actually a preamble to the second convention, which would seem, therefore, to take the place of the first. As a matter of fact, the discussion is a barren one, since both parties agree that Great Britain retained certain rights over the making of treaties by the Republic, which rights place her in a different position to an entirely independent state. Whether this difference amounts to a suzerainty or not is a subject for the academic discussion of international jurists. What is of importance is the fact, not the word.

II. THE CAUSE OF QUARREL

Gold had been known to exist in the Transvaal before, but it was only in 1886 that it was realised that the deposits which lie some thirty miles south of the capital are of a very extraordinary and valuable nature. The proportion of gold in the quartz is not particularly high, nor are the veins of a remarkable thickness, but the peculiarity of the Rand mines lies in the fact that throughout this 'banket' formation the metal is so uniformly distributed that the enterprise can claim a certainty which is not usually associated with the industry. It is quarrying rather than mining. Add to this that the reefs which were originally worked as outcrops have now been traced to enormous depths, and present the same features as those at the surface. A conservative estimate of the value of the gold has placed it at seven hundred millions of pounds.

Such a discovery produced the inevitable effect. A great number of adventurers flocked into the country, some desirable and some very much the reverse. There were circumstances, however, which kept away the rowdy and desperado element who usually make for a newly-opened goldfield. It was not a class of mining which encouraged the individual adventurer. It was a field for elaborate machinery, which could only be provided by capital. Managers, engineers, miners, technical experts, and the tradesmen and middlemen who live upon them, these were the Uitlanders, drawn from all races under the sun, but with the Anglo-Celtic vastly predominant. The best engineers were American, the best miners were Cornish, the best managers were English, the money to run the mines was largely subscribed in England. As time went on, however, the German and French interests became more extensive, until their joint holdings are now probably as heavy as those of the British. Soon the population of the mining centres became about as numerous as that of the whole Boer community, and consisted mainly of men in the prime of life—men, too, of exceptional intelligence and energy.

The situation was an extraordinary one. I have already attempted to bring the problem home to an American by suggesting that the Dutch of New York had trekked west and founded an anti-American and highly unprogressive State. To carry out the analogy we will now suppose that that State was California, that the gold of that State attracted a large inrush of American citizens, that these citizens were heavily taxed and badly used, and that they deafened Washington with their outcry about their injuries. That would be a fair parallel to the relations between the Transvaal, the Uitlanders, and the British Government.

That these Uitlanders had very real and pressing grievances no one could possibly deny. To recount them all would be a formidable task, for their whole lives were darkened by injustice. There was not a wrong which had driven the Boer from Cape Colony which he did not now practise himself upon others—and a wrong may be excusable in 1835 which is monstrous in 1895. The primitive virtue which had characterised the farmers broke down in the face of temptation. The country Boers were little affected, some of them not at all, but the Pretoria Government became a most corrupt oligarchy, venal and incompetent to the last degree. Officials and imported Hollanders handled the stream of gold which came in from the mines, while the unfortunate Uitlander who paid nine-tenths of the taxation was fleeced at every turn, and met with laughter and taunts when he endeavoured to win the franchise by which he might peaceably set right the wrongs from which he suffered. He was not an unreasonable person. On the contrary, he was patient to the verge of meekness, as capital is likely to be when it is surrounded by rifles. But his situation was intolerable, and after successive attempts at peaceful agitation, and numerous humble petitions to the Volksraad, he began at last to realise that he would never obtain redress unless he could find some way of winning it for himself.

Without attempting to enumerate all the wrongs which embittered the Uitlanders, the more serious of them may be summed up in this way:

1. That they were heavily taxed and provided about seven-eighths of the revenue of the country. The revenue of the South African Republic—which had been 154,000£. in 1886, when the goldfields were opened—had grown in 1899 to four million pounds, and the country through the industry of the new-comers had changed from one of the poorest to the richest in the whole world (per head of population).

2. That in spite of this prosperity which they had brought, they were left without a vote, and could by no means influence the disposal of the great sums which they were

providing. Such a case of taxation without representation has never been known.

3. That they had no voice in the choice or payment of officials. Men of the worst private character might be placed with complete authority over valuable interests. The total official salaries had risen in 1899 to a sum sufficient to pay 40£. per head to the entire male Boer population.

4. That they had no control over education. Mr. John Robinson, the Director-General of the Johannesburg Educational Council, has reckoned the sum spent on the Uitlander schools as 650£. out of 63,000£ allotted for education, making 1s.10d. per head per annum on Uitlander children, and 8£ 6s. per head on Boer children—the Uitlander, as always, paying seven-eighths of the original sum.

5. No power of municipal government. Watercarts instead of pipes, filthy buckets instead of drains, a corrupt and violent police, a high death-rate in what should be a health resort—all this in a city which they had built themselves.

6. Despotic government in the matter of the Press and of the right of public meeting.

7. Disability from service upon a jury.

8. Continual harassing of the mining interest by vexatious legislation. Under this head come many grievances, some special to the mines and some affecting all Uitlanders. The dynamite monopoly, by which the miners had to pay 600,000£. extra per annum in order to get a worse quality of dynamite; the liquor laws, by which the Kaffirs were allowed to be habitually drunk; the incompetence and extortions of the State-owned railway; the granting of concessions for numerous articles of ordinary consumption

to individuals, by which high prices were maintained; the surrounding of Johannesburg by tolls from which the town had no profit—these were among the economical grievances, some large, some petty, which ramified through every transaction of life. These are the wrongs which Mr. W. T. Stead has described as 'the twopenny-halfpenny grievances of a handful of Englishmen.'

The manner in which the blood was sucked from the Uitlanders, and the rapid spread of wealth among the Boer officials, may be gathered from the list of the salaries of the State servants from the opening of the mines to the outbreak of the war:

Year	£
1886	51,831
1887	99,083
1888	164,466
1889	249,641
1890	324,520
1891	332,888
1892	323,608
1893	361,275
1894	419,775
1895	570,047
1896	813,029
1897	996,959
1898	1,080,382
1899	1,216,394

which shows, as Mr. FitzPatrick has pointed out, that the salary list had become twenty-four times what it was when the Uitlanders arrived, and five times as much as the total revenue was then.

But outside and beyond all the definite wrongs from which they suffered, there was a constant irritation to freeborn and progressive men, accustomed to liberal institutions, that they should be despotically ruled by a body of men some of whom were ignorant bigots, some of them buffoons, and nearly all of them openly and shamelessly corrupt. Out of twenty-five members of the First Volksraad twenty-one were, in the case of the Selati Railway Company, publicly and circumstantially accused of bribery, with full details of the bribes received, their date, and who paid them. The black-list includes the present vice-president, Schalk Burger; the vice-president of that date; Eloff, the son-in-law of Kruger; and the secretary of the Volksraad. Apparently every man of the executive and the legislature had his price.

A corrupt assembly is an evil master, but when it is narrow-minded and bigoted as well, it becomes indeed intolerable. The following tit-bits from the debates in the two Raads show the intelligence and spirit of the men who were ruling over one of the most progressive communities in the world:

'Pillar-boxes in Pretoria were opposed on the grounds that they were extravagant and effeminate. Deputy Taljaard said that he could not see why people wanted to be always writing letters; he wrote none himself. In the days of his youth he had written a letter and had not been afraid to travel fifty miles and more on horseback and by wagon to post it—and now people complained if they had to go one mile.'

A debate on the possibility of decreasing the plague of locusts led to the following enlightened discussion:

'*July 21.*—Mr. Roos said locusts were a plague, as in the days of King Pharaoh, sent by God, and the country would assuredly be loaded with shame and obloquy if it tried to raise its hand against the mighty hand of the Almighty.

'Messrs. Declerq and Steenkamp spoke in the same strain, quoting largely from the Scriptures.

'The Chairman related a true story of a man whose farm was always spared by the locusts, until one day he caused some to be killed. His farm was then devastated.

'Mr. Stoop conjured the members not to constitute themselves terrestrial gods and oppose the Almighty.

'Mr. Lucas Meyer raised a storm by ridiculing the arguments of the former speakers, and comparing the locusts to beasts of prey which they destroyed.

'Mr. Labuschagne was violent. He said the locusts were quite different from beasts of prey. They were a special plague sent by God for their sinfulness.'

In a further debate:

'Mr. Jan de Beer complained of the lack of uniformity in neckties. Some wore a Tom Thumb variety, and others wore scarves. This was a state of things to be deplored, and he considered that the Raad should put its foot down and define the size and shape of neckties.'

The following note of a debate gives some idea of how far the legislators were qualified to deal with commercial questions:

'*May 8.*—On the application of the Sheba G. M. Co. for permission to erect an aerial tram from the mine to the mill,

'Mr. Grobelaar asked whether an aerial tram was a balloon or whether it could fly through the air.

'The only objection that the Chairman had to urge against granting the tram was that the Company had an English name, and that with so many Dutch ones available.

'Mr. Taljaard objected to the word "participeeren" (participate) as not being Dutch, and to him unintelligible: "I can't believe the word is Dutch; why have I never come across it in the Bible if it is?"

'*June 18.*—On the application for a concession to treat tailings,

'Mr. Taljaard wished to know if the words "pyrites" and "concentrates" could not be translated into the Dutch language. He could not understand what it meant. He had gone to night-school as long as he had been in Pretoria, and even now he could not explain everything to his burghers. He thought it a shame that big hills should be made on ground under which there might be rich reefs, and which in future might be required for a market or outspan. He would support the recommendation on condition that the name of the quartz should be translated into Dutch, as there might be more in this than some of them imagined.'

Such debates as these may be amusing at a distance, but they are less entertaining when they come from an autocrat who has complete power over the conditions of your life.

From the fact that they were a community extremely preoccupied by their own business, it followed that the Uitlanders were not ardent politicians, and that they desired to have a share in the government of the State for the purpose of making the conditions of their own industry and of their own daily lives more endurable. How far there was need of such an interference may be judged by any fair-minded man who reads the list of their complaints. A superficial view may recognise the Boers as the champions of liberty, but a deeper insight must see that they (as represented by their elected rulers) have in truth stood for all that history has shown to be odious in the form of exclusiveness and oppression. Their conception of liberty has been a narrow and selfish one, and they have consistently inflicted upon others far heavier wrongs than those against which they had themselves rebelled.

As the mines increased in importance and the miners in numbers, it was found that these political disabilities affected some of that cosmopolitan crowd far more than others, in proportion to the amount of freedom to which their home institutions had made them accustomed. The Continental Uitlanders were more patient of that which was unendurable to the American and the Briton. The Americans, however, were in so great a minority that it was upon the British that the brunt of the struggle for freedom fell. Apart from the fact that the British were more numerous than all the other Uitlanders combined, there were special reasons why they should feel their humiliating position more than the members of any other race. In the first place, many of the British were British South Africans, who knew that in the neighbouring countries which gave them birth the most liberal possible institutions had been given to the kinsmen of these very Boers who were refusing them the management of their own drains and water-supply. And again, every Briton knew that Great Britain claimed to be the paramount Power in South Africa, and so he felt as if his own land, to which he might have looked for protection, was conniving at and acquiescing in his ill-treatment. As citizens of the paramount Power, it was peculiarly galling that they should be held in political subjection. The British, therefore, were the most persistent and energetic of the agitators.

But it is a poor cause which cannot bear to fairly state and honestly consider the case of its opponents. The Boers had made, as has been briefly shown, great efforts to establish a country of their own. They had travelled far, worked hard, and fought bravely. After all their efforts they were fated to see an influx of strangers into their country, some of them men of questionable character, who threatened to outnumber the original inhabitants. If the franchise were granted to these, there could be no doubt that, though at first the Boers might control a majority of the votes, it was only a question of time before the new-comers would dominate the Raad and elect their own President, who might adopt a policy abhorrent to the original owners of the land. Were the Boers to lose by the ballot-box the victory which they had won by their rifles? Was it fair to expect it? These new-comers came for gold. They got their gold. Their companies paid a hundred per cent. Was not that enough to satisfy them? If they did not like the country, why did they not leave it? No one compelled them to stay there. But if they stayed, let them be thankful that they were tolerated at all, and not presume to interfere with the laws of those by whose courtesy they were allowed to enter the country.

That is a fair statement of the Boer position, and at first sight an impartial man might say that there was a good deal to say for it; but a closer examination would show that, though it might be tenable in theory, it is unjust and impossible in practice.

In the present crowded state of the world a policy of Thibet may be carried out in some obscure corner, but it cannot be done in a great tract of country which lies right across the main line of industrial progress. The position is too absolutely artificial. A handful of people by the right of conquest take possession of an enormous country over which they are dotted at such intervals that it is their boast that one farmhouse cannot see the smoke of another, and yet, though their numbers are so disproportionate to the area which they cover, they refuse to admit any other people upon equal terms, but claim to be a privileged class who shall dominate the new-comers completely. They are outnumbered in their own land by immigrants who are far more highly educated and progressive, and yet they hold them down in a way which exists nowhere else upon earth. What is their right? The right of conquest. Then the same right may be justly invoked to reverse so intolerable a situation. This they would themselves acknowledge. 'Come on and fight! Come on!' cried a member of the Volksraad when the franchise petition of the Uitlanders was presented. 'Protest! Protest! What is the good of protesting?' said Kruger to Mr. W. Y. Campbell; 'you have not got the guns, I have.' There was always the final court of appeal. Judge Creusot and Judge Mauser were always behind the President.

Again, the argument of the Boers would be more valid had they received no benefit from these immigrants. If they had ignored them they might fairly have stated that they did not desire their presence. But even while they protested they grew rich at the Uitlanders' expense. They could not have it both ways. It would be consistent to discourage him and not profit by him, or to make him comfortable and build the State upon his money; but to ill-treat him and at the same time grow strong by his taxation must surely be an injustice.

And again, the whole argument is based upon the narrow racial supposition that every naturalised citizen not of Boer extraction must necessarily be unpatriotic. This is not borne out by the examples of history. The new-comer soon becomes as proud of his country and as jealous of her liberty as the old. Had President Kruger given the franchise generously to the Uitlander, his pyramid would have been firm upon its base and not balanced upon its apex. It is true that the corrupt oligarchy would have vanished, and the spirit of a broader, more tolerant freedom influenced the counsels of the State. But the republic would have become stronger and more permanent with a population who, if they differed in details, were united in essentials. Whether such a solution would have been to the advantage of British interests in South Africa is quite another question. In more ways than one President Kruger has been a good friend to the Empire.

At the time of the Convention of Pretoria (1881) the rights of burghership might be obtained by one year's residence. In 1882 it was raised to five years, the reasonable limit which obtains both in Great Britain and in the United States. Had it remained so, it is safe to say that there would never have been either an Uitlander question or a war. Grievances would have been righted from the inside without external interference.

In 1890 the inrush of outsiders alarmed the Boers, and the franchise was raised so as to be only attainable by those who had lived fourteen years in the country. The Uitlanders, who were increasing rapidly in numbers and were suffering from the formidable list of grievances already enumerated, perceived that their wrongs were so numerous that it was hopeless to have them set right seriatim, and that only by obtaining the leverage of the franchise could they hope to move the heavy burden which weighed them down. In 1893 a petition of 13,000 Uitlanders, couched in most respectful terms, was submitted to the Raad, but met with contemptuous neglect. Undeterred, however, by this failure, the National Reform Union, an association which was not one of capitalists, came back to the attack in 1894. They drew up a petition which was signed by 35,000 adult male Uitlanders, as great a number probably as the total Boer male population of the country. A small liberal body in the Raad supported this memorial and endeavoured in vain to obtain some justice for the new-comers. Mr. Jeppe was the mouthpiece of this select band. 'They own half the soil, they pay at least three-quarters of the taxes,' said he. 'They are men who in capital, energy, and education are at least our equals. What will become of us or our children on that day when we may find ourselves in a minority of one in twenty without a single friend among the other nineteen, among those who will then tell us that they wished to be brothers, but that we by our own act have made them strangers to the republic?' Such reasonable and liberal sentiments were combated by members who asserted that the signatures could not belong to law-abiding citizens, since they were actually agitating against the law of the franchise, and others whose intolerance was expressed by the defiance of the member already quoted, who challenged the Uitlanders to come out and fight. The champions of exclusiveness and racial hatred won the day. The memorial was rejected by sixteen votes to eight, and the franchise law was, on the initiative of the President, actually made more stringent than ever, being framed in such a way that during the fourteen years of probation the applicant should give up his previous nationality, so that for that period he would belong to no country at all. No hopes were held out that any possible attitude upon the part of the Uitlanders would soften the determination of the President and his burghers. One who remonstrated was led outside the State buildings by the President, who pointed up at the national flag. 'You see that flag?' said he. 'If I grant the franchise, I may as well pull it down.' His animosity against the immigrants was bitter. 'Burghers, friends, thieves, murderers, new- comers, and others,' is the conciliatory opening of one of his public addresses. Though Johannesburg is only thirty-two miles from Pretoria, and though the State of which he was the head depended for its revenue upon the goldfields, he paid it only three visits in nine years.

This settled animosity was deplorable, but not unnatural. A man imbued with the idea of a chosen people, and unread in any book save the one which cultivates this very idea, could not be expected to have learned the historical lessons of the advantages which a State reaps from a liberal policy. To him it was as if the Ammonites and Moabites had demanded admission into the twelve tribes. He mistook an agitation against the exclusive policy of the State for one against the existence of the State itself. A wide franchise would have made his republic firm-based and permanent. It was a minority of the Uitlanders who had any desire to come into the British system. They were a cosmopolitan crowd, only united by the bond of a common injustice. The majority of the British immigrants had no desire to subvert the State. But when every other method had failed, and their petition for the rights of freemen had been flung back at them, it was natural that their eyes should turn to that flag which waved to the north, the west, and the south of them—the flag which means purity of government with equal rights and equal duties for all men. Constitutional agitation was laid aside, arms were smuggled in, and everything prepared for an organised rising.

It had been arranged that the town was to rise upon a certain night, that Pretoria should be attacked, the fort seized, and the rifles and ammunition, used to arm the Uitlanders. It was a feasible device, though it must seem to us, who have had such an experience of the military virtues of the burghers, a very desperate one. But it is conceivable that the rebels might have held Johannesburg until the universal sympathy which their cause excited throughout South Africa would have caused Great Britain to intervene. Unfortunately they had complicated matters by asking for outside help. Mr. Cecil Rhodes was Premier of the Cape, a man of immense energy, and one who had rendered great services to the empire. The motives of his action are obscure—certainly, we may say that they were not sordid, for he has always been a man whose thoughts were large and whose habits were simple. But whatever they may have been—whether an ill-regulated desire to consolidate South Africa under British rule, or a burning sympathy with the Uitlanders in their fight against injustice—it is certain that he allowed his lieutenant, Dr. Jameson, to assemble the mounted police of the Chartered Company, of which Rhodes was founder and director, for the purpose of co-operating with the rebels at Johannesburg. Moreover, when the revolt at Johannesburg was postponed, on account of a disagreement as to which flag they were to rise under, it appears that Jameson (with or without the orders of Rhodes) forced the hand of the conspirators by invading the country with a force absurdly inadequate to the work which he had taken in hand. Five hundred policemen and two field-guns made up the forlorn hope who started from near Mafeking and crossed the Transvaal border upon December 29, 1895. On January 2 they were surrounded by the Boers amid the broken country near Dornkop, and after losing many of their number killed and wounded, without food and with spent horses, they were compelled to lay down their arms. Six burghers lost their lives in the skirmish.

Determined attempts have been made to connect the British Government with this fiasco, and to pretend that the Colonial Secretary and other statesmen were cognisant of it. Such an impression has been fostered by the apparent reluctance of the Commission of Inquiry to push their researches to the uttermost. It is much to be regretted that every possible telegram and letter should not have been called for upon that occasion; but the idea that this was not done for fear that Mr. Chamberlain and the British Government would be implicated, becomes absurd in the presence of the fact that the Commission included among its members Sir Henry Campbell-Bannerman and Sir William Harcourt. Is it conceivable that these gentlemen held their hands for fear of damaging the Government, or that Mr. Chamberlain could afterwards have the effrontery to publicly and solemnly deny all knowledge of the business in the presence of gentlemen who had connived at the suppression of the proofs that he *did* know? Such a supposition is ridiculous, and yet it is involved in the theory that the Commission refrained from pushing their examination because they were afraid of showing their country to have been in the wrong.

Again, even the most embittered enemy of Mr. Chamberlain must admit that he is a clear-headed man, a man of resolution, and a man with some sense of proportion as to the means which should be used for an end. Is such a man, knowing the military record of the burghers, the sort of man to connive at the invasion of their country by 500 policemen and two guns? Would he be likely, even if he approved of the general aim, to sanction such a harebrained piece of folly? And, having sanctioned it, would he be so weak of purpose as to take energetic steps, the instant that he heard of the invasion, to undo that which he is supposed himself to have done, and to cause the failure of his own scheme? Why should he on such a supposition send energetic messages to Johannesburg forbidding the British to co-operate with the raiders? The whole accusation is so absurd that it is only the mania of party spite or of national hatred which could induce anyone to believe it.

Again, supposing for an instant that the British Government knew anything about the coming raid, what is the first and most obvious thing which they would have done? Whether Jameson got safely to Johannesburg or not there was evidently a probability of a great race-struggle in South Africa. Would they not then, on some pretext or another, have increased the strength of the British force in the country, which was so weak that it was powerless to influence the course of events? It is certain that this is so. But nothing of the kind was done.

Mr. Chamberlain's own denial is clear and emphatic:

'I desire to say in the most explicit manner that I had not then, and that I never had, any knowledge, or until, I think it was the day before the actual raid took place, the slightest suspicion of anything in the nature of a hostile or armed invasion of the Transvaal.' — (British South Africa Committee, 1897. Q. 6223.)

The Earl of Selborne, Under-Secretary of State for the Colonies, was no less explicit:

'Neither then nor at any subsequent period prior to the raid did we know of what is now called "Jameson's plan," nor that the revolution at Johannesburg was being largely controlled and financed from Cape Colony and Rhodesia.... Sir Hercules Robinson had no suspicion of what was impending, nor apparently President Kruger, nor Mr. Hofmeyr, nor any public man in South Africa, except those who were preparing the plan. At any rate the fact remains that from no quarter did the Colonial Office receive any warning. I submit, therefore, it would have been a most extraordinary thing if any suspicion had occurred to us.'

The finding of the Committee—a Committee composed of men of all parties, some of whom, as we know, were yearning 'to give Joe a fall'—was unanimous in condemning the raid and equally unanimous in exonerating the Government from any knowledge of it. Their Report said:

'Your Committee fully accept the statements of the Secretary of State for the Colonies, and of the Under-Secretary, and entirely exonerate the officials of the Colonial Office of having been in any sense cognisant of the plans which led up to the incursion of Dr. Jameson's force into the South African Republic....

'Neither the Secretary of State for the Colonies, nor any of the officials of the Colonial Office received any information which made them, or should have made them, or any of them, aware of the plot during its development.'

And yet to this day it is one of the articles of faith of a few crack-brained fanatics in this country, and of many ill-informed and prejudiced editors upon the Continent, that the British Government was responsible for the raid.

The Uitlanders have been severely criticised for not having sent out a force to help Jameson in his difficulties, but it is impossible to see how they could have acted in any other manner. They had done all they could to prevent Jameson coming to their relief, and now it was rather unreasonable to suppose that they should relieve their reliever. Indeed, they had an entirely exaggerated idea of the strength of the force which he was bringing, and received the news of his capture with incredulity. When it became confirmed they rose, but in a half-hearted fashion which was not due to want of courage, but to the difficulties of their position. On the one hand the British Government disowned Jameson entirely, and did all it could to discourage the rising; on the other, the President had the raiders in his keeping at Pretoria, and let it be understood that their fate depended upon the behaviour of the Uitlanders. They were led to believe that Jameson would be shot unless they laid down their arms, though, as a matter of fact, Jameson and his people had surrendered upon a promise of quarter. So skilfully did Kruger use his hostages that he succeeded, with the help of the British Commissioner, in getting the thousands of excited Johannesburgers to lay down their arms without bloodshed. Completely out-manoeuvred by the astute old President, the leaders of the reform movement used all their influence in the direction of peace, thinking that a general amnesty would follow; but the moment that they and their people were helpless the detectives and armed burghers occupied the town, and sixty of their number were hurried to Pretoria Gaol.

To the raiders themselves the President behaved with generosity. Perhaps he could not find it in his heart to be harsh to the men who had managed to put him in the right and won for him the sympathy of the world. His own illiberal and oppressive treatment of the new-comers was forgotten in the face of this illegal inroad of filibusters. The true issues were so obscured by this intrusion that it has taken years to clear them, and perhaps they will never be wholly cleared. It was forgotten that it was the bad government of the country which was the real cause of the unfortunate raid. From then onwards the government might grow worse and worse, but it was always possible to point to the raid as justifying everything. Were the Uitlanders to have the franchise? How could they expect it after the raid? Would Britain object to the enormous importation of arms and obvious preparations for war? They were only precautions against a second raid. For years the raid stood in the way, not only of all progress, but of all remonstrance. Through an action over which they had no control, and which they had done their best to prevent, the British Government was left with a bad case and a weakened moral authority.

The raiders were sent home, where the rank and file were very properly released, and the chief officers were condemned to terms of imprisonment which certainly did not err upon the side of severity. In the meantime, both President Kruger and his burghers had shown a greater severity to the political prisoners from Johannesburg than to the armed followers of Jameson. The nationality of these prisoners is interesting and suggestive. There were twenty-three Englishmen, sixteen South Africans, nine Scotchmen, six Americans, two Welshmen, one Irishman, one Australian, one Hollander, one Bavarian, one Canadian, one Swiss, and one Turk. The list is sufficient comment upon the assertion that only the British Uitlanders made serious complaints of subjection and injustice. The prisoners were arrested in January, but the trial did not take place until the end of April. All were found guilty of high treason. Mr. Lionel Phillips, Colonel Rhodes (brother of Mr. Cecil Rhodes), George Farrar, and Mr. Hammond, the American engineer, were condemned to death, a sentence which was afterwards commuted to the payment of an enormous fine. The other prisoners were condemned to two years' imprisonment, with a fine of 2,000£. each. The imprisonment was of the most arduous and trying sort, and was embittered by the harshness of the gaoler, Du Plessis. One of the unfortunate men cut his throat, and several fell seriously ill, the diet and the sanitary conditions being equally unhealthy. At last, at the end of May, all the prisoners but six were released. Four of the six soon followed, two stalwarts, Sampson and Davies, refusing to sign any petition and remaining in prison until they were set free in 1897. Altogether the Transvaal Government received in fines from the reform prisoners the enormous sum of 212,000£. A certain comic relief was immediately afterwards given to so grave an episode by the presentation of a bill to Great Britain for 1,677,938£.3s.3d. — the greater part of which was under the heading of moral and intellectual damage. It is to be feared that even the 3s. 3d. remains still unpaid.

The raid was past and the reform movement was past, but the causes which produced them both remained. It is hardly conceivable that a statesman who loved his country would have refrained from making some effort to remove a state of things which had already caused such grave dangers, and which must obviously become more serious with every year that passed. But Paul Kruger had hardened his heart, and was not to be moved. The grievances of the Uitlanders became heavier than ever. The one power in the land to which they had been able to appeal for some sort of redress amid their troubles was the law courts. Now it was decreed that the courts should be dependent on the Volksraad. The Chief Justice protested against such a degradation of his high office, and he was dismissed in consequence without a pension. The judge who had condemned the reformers was chosen to fill the vacancy, and the protection of a fixed law was withdrawn from the Uitlanders.

A commission appointed by the State was sent to examine into the condition of the mining industry and the grievances from which the new-comers suffered. The chairman was Mr. Schalk Burger, one of the most liberal of the Boers, and the proceedings were thorough and impartial. The result was a report which amply vindicated the reformers, and suggested remedies which would have gone a long way towards satisfying the Uitlanders. With such enlightened legislation their motives for seeking the franchise would have been less pressing. But the President and his Raad would have none of the recommendations of the commission. The rugged old autocrat declared that Schalk Burger was a traitor to his country for having signed such a document, and a new reactionary committee was chosen to report upon the report. Words and papers were the only outcome of the affair. No amelioration came to the new-comers. But at least they had again put their case publicly upon record, and it had been endorsed by the most respected of the burghers. Gradually in the press of the English-speaking countries the raid was ceasing to obscure the issue. More and more clearly it was coming out that no permanent settlement was possible where half the population was oppressed by the other half. They had tried peaceful means and failed. They had tried warlike means and failed. What was there left for them to do? Their own country, the paramount power of South Africa, had never helped them. Perhaps if it were directly appealed to it might do so. It could not, if only for the sake of its own imperial prestige, leave its children for ever in a state of subjection. The small spark which caused a final explosion came from the shooting of a British subject named Edgar by a Boer policeman, Jones, in Johannesburg. The action of the policeman was upheld by the authorities, and the British felt that their lives were no longer safe in the presence of an armed overbearing police. At another time the incident might have been of no great importance, but at that moment it seemed to be taken as the crowning example of the injustice under which the miners suffered. A meeting of protest called by the British residents was broken up by gangs of workmen under Boer officials. Driven to desperation the Uitlanders determined upon a petition to Queen Victoria, and in doing so they brought their grievances out of the limits of a local controversy into the broader field of international politics. Great Britain must either protect them or acknowledge that their protection was beyond her power. A direct petition to the Queen praying for protection was signed in April 1899 by 21,000 Uitlanders.

The lines which this historical petition took may be judged from the following excerpt:

'The condition of Your Majesty's subjects in this State has indeed become well-nigh intolerable.

'The acknowledged and admitted grievances of which Your Majesty's subjects complained prior to 1895, not only are not redressed, but exist to-day in an aggravated form. They are still deprived of all political rights, they are denied any voice in the government of the country, they are taxed far above the requirements of the country, the revenue of which is misapplied and devoted to objects which keep alive a continuous and well-founded feeling of irritation, without in any way advancing the general interest of the State. Maladministration and peculation of public moneys go hand-in-hand, without any vigorous measures being adopted to put a stop to the scandal. The education of Uitlander children is made subject to impossible conditions. The police afford no adequate protection to the lives and property of the inhabitants of Johannesburg; they are rather a source of danger to the peace and safety of the Uitlander population.

'A further grievance has become prominent since the beginning of the year. The power vested in the Government by means of the Public Meetings Act has been a menace to Your Majesty's subjects since the enactment of the Act in 1894. This power has now been applied in order to deliver a blow that strikes at the inherent and inalienable birthright of every British subject—namely, his right to petition his Sovereign. Straining to the utmost the language and intention of the law, the Government have arrested two British subjects who assisted in presenting a petition to Your Majesty on behalf of four thousand fellow-subjects. Not content with this, the Government, when Your Majesty's loyal subjects again attempted to lay their grievances before Your Majesty, permitted their meeting to be broken up, and the objects of it to be defeated, by a body of Boers, organised by Government officials and acting under the protection of the police. By reason, therefore, of the direct, as well as the indirect, act of the Government, Your Majesty's loyal subjects have been prevented from publicly ventilating their grievances, and from laying them before Your Majesty.

'Wherefore Your Majesty's humble petitioners humbly beseech Your Most Gracious Majesty to extend Your Majesty's protection to Your Majesty's loyal subjects resident in this State, and to cause an inquiry to be made into grievances and complaints enumerated and set forth in this humble petition, and to direct Your Majesty's representative in South Africa to take measures which will insure the speedy reform of the abuses complained of, and to obtain substantial guarantees from the Government of this State for a recognition of their rights as British subjects.'

From the date of this direct petition from our ill-used people to their Sovereign events moved inevitably towards one end. Sometimes the surface was troubled and sometimes smooth, but the stream always ran swiftly and the roar of the fall sounded ever louder in the ears.

III. THE NEGOTIATIONS

The British Government and the British people do not desire any direct authority in South Africa. Their one supreme interest is that the various States there should live in concord and prosperity, and that there should be no need for the presence of a British redcoat within the whole great peninsula. Our foreign critics, with their misapprehension of the British colonial system, can never realise that whether the four-coloured flag of the Transvaal or the Union Jack of a self-governing colony waved over the gold mines would not make the difference of one shilling to the revenue of Great Britain. The Transvaal as a British province would have its own legislature, its own revenue, its own expenditure, and its own tariff against the mother country, as well as against the rest of the world, and Britain be none the richer for the change. This is so obvious to a

Briton that he has ceased to insist upon it, and it is for that reason perhaps that it is so universally misunderstood abroad. On the other hand, while she is no gainer by the change, most of the expense of it in blood and in money falls upon the home country. On the face of it, therefore, Great Britain had every reason to avoid so formidable a task as the conquest of the South African Republic. At the best she had nothing to gain, and at the worst she had an immense deal to lose. There was no room for ambition or aggression. It was a case of shirking or fulfilling a most arduous duty.

There could be no question of a plot for the annexation of the Transvaal. In a free country the Government cannot move in advance of public opinion, and public opinion is influenced by and reflected in the newspapers. One may examine the files of the press during all the months of negotiations and never find one reputable opinion in favour of such a course, nor did one in society ever meet an advocate of such a measure. But a great wrong was being done, and all that was asked was the minimum change which would set it right, and restore equality between the white races in Africa. 'Let Kruger only be liberal in the extension of the franchise,' said the paper which is most representative of the sanest British opinion, 'and he will find that the power of the republic will become not weaker, but infinitely more secure. Let him once give the majority of the resident males of full age the full vote, and he will have given the republic a stability and power which nothing else can. If he rejects all pleas of this kind, and persists in his present policy, he may possibly stave off the evil day, and preserve his cherished oligarchy for another few years; but the end will be the same.' The extract reflects the tone of all the British press with the exception of one or two papers which considered that even the persistent ill-usage of our people, and the fact that we were peculiarly responsible for them in this State, did not justify us in interfering in the internal affairs of the republic. It cannot be denied that the Jameson Raid had weakened the force of those who wished to interfere energetically on behalf of British subjects. There was a vague but widespread feeling that perhaps the capitalists were engineering the situation for their own ends. It is difficult to imagine how a state of unrest and insecurity, to say nothing of a state of war, can ever be to the advantage of capital, and surely it is obvious that if some arch-schemer were using the grievances of the Uitlanders for his own ends the best way to checkmate him would be to remove those grievances. The suspicion, however, did exist among those who like to ignore the obvious and magnify the remote, and throughout the negotiations the hand of Great Britain was weakened, as her adversary had doubtless calculated that it would be, by an earnest but fussy and faddy minority.

It was in April 1899 that the British Uitlanders sent their petition praying for protection to their native country. Since the April previous a correspondence had been going on between Dr. Leyds, Secretary of State for the South African Republic, and Mr. Chamberlain, Colonial Secretary, upon the existence or non-existence of the suzerainty. On the one hand, it was contended that the substitution of a second convention had entirely annulled the first; on the other, that the preamble of the first applied also to the second. If the Transvaal contention were correct it is clear that Great Britain had been tricked and jockeyed into such a position, since she had received no *quid pro quo* in the second convention, and even the most careless of Colonial Secretaries could hardly have been expected to give away a very substantial something for nothing. But the contention throws us back upon the academic question of what a suzerainty is. The Transvaal admitted a power of veto over their foreign policy, and this admission in itself, unless they openly tore up the convention, must deprive them of the position of a sovereign State.

But now to this debate, which had so little of urgency in it that seven months intervened between statement and reply, there came the bitterly vital question of the wrongs and appeal of the Uitlanders. Sir Alfred Milner, the British Commissioner in South Africa, a man of liberal politics who had been appointed by a Conservative Government, commanded the respect and confidence of all parties. His record was that of an able, clear-headed man, too just to be either guilty of or tolerant of injustice. To him the matter was referred, and a conference was arranged between President Kruger and him at Bloemfontein, the capital of the Orange Free State. They met on May 31, 1899.

There were three different classes of subject which had to be discussed at the Conference. One included all those alleged breaches of the Convention of London which had caused so much friction between the two Governments, and which had thrice in eighteen years brought the States to the verge of war. Among these subjects would be the Boer annexations of native territory, such interference with trade as the stopping of the Drifts, the question of suzerainty, and the possibility of arbitration. The second class of questions would deal with the grievances of the Uitlanders, which presented a problem which had in no way been provided for in the Conventions. The third class contained the question of the ill-treatment of British Indians, and other causes of quarrel. Sir Alfred Milner was faced with the alternative either to argue over each of these questions in turn—an endless and unprofitable business—or to put forward some one test-question which would strike at the root of the matter and prove whether a real attempt would be made by the Boer Government to relieve the tension. The question which he selected was that of the franchise for the

Uitlanders, for it was evident that if they obtained not a fair share—such a request was never made—but any appreciable share in the government of the country, they would in time be able to relieve their own grievances and so spare the British Government the heavy task of acting as their champions. But the Conference was quickly wrecked upon this question. Milner contended for a five years' retroactive franchise, with provisions to secure adequate representation for the mining districts. Kruger offered a seven-years' franchise, coupled with numerous conditions which whittled down its value very much; promised five members out of thirty-one to represent half the male adult population; and added a provision that all differences should be subject to arbitration by foreign powers—a condition which is incompatible with any claim to suzerainty. This offer dropped the term for the franchise from fourteen years to seven, but it retained a number of conditions which might make it illusory, while demanding in exchange a most important concession from the British Government. The proposals of each were impossible to the other, and early in June Sir Alfred Milner was back in Cape Town and President Kruger in Pretoria, with nothing settled except the extreme difficulty of a settlement.

On June 12 Sir Alfred Milner received a deputation at Cape Town and reviewed the situation. 'The principle of equality of races was,' he said, 'essential for South Africa. The one State where inequality existed kept all the others in a fever. Our policy was one not of aggression, but of singular patience, which could not, however, lapse into indifference.' Two days later Kruger addressed the Raad. 'The other side had not conceded one tittle, and I could not give more. God has always stood by us. I do not want war, but I will not give more away. Although our independence has once been taken away, God had restored it.' He spoke with sincerity no doubt, but it is hard to hear God invoked with such confidence for the system which encouraged the liquor traffic to the natives, and bred the most corrupt set of officials that the modern world has seen.

A despatch from Sir Alfred Milner, giving his views upon the situation, made the British public recognise, as nothing else had done, how serious the position was, and how essential it was that an earnest national effort should be made to set it right. In it he said:

'The case for intervention is overwhelming. The only attempted answer is that things will right themselves if left alone. But, in fact, the policy of leaving things alone has been tried for years, and it has led to their going from bad to worse. It is not true that this is owing to the raid. They were going from bad to worse before the raid. We were on the verge of war before the raid, and the Transvaal was on the verge of revolution. The effect of the raid has been to give the policy of leaving things alone a new lease of life, and with the old consequences.

'The spectacle of thousands of British subjects kept permanently in the position of helots, constantly chafing under undoubted grievances, and calling vainly to her Majesty's Government for redress, does steadily undermine the influence and reputation of Great Britain within the Queen's dominions. A section of the press, not in the Transvaal only, preaches openly and constantly the doctrine of a republic embracing all South Africa, and supports it by menacing references to the armaments of the Transvaal, its alliance with the Orange Free State, and the active sympathy which, in case of war, it would receive from a section of her Majesty's subjects. I regret to say that this doctrine, supported as it is by a ceaseless stream of malignant lies about the intentions of her Majesty's Government, is producing a great effect on a large number of our Dutch fellow-colonists. Language is frequently used which seems to imply that the Dutch have some superior right, even in this colony, to their fellow-citizens of British birth. Thousands of men peaceably disposed, and if left alone perfectly satisfied with their position as British subjects, are being drawn into disaffection, and there is a corresponding exasperation upon the part of the British.

'I can see nothing which will put a stop to this mischievous propaganda but some striking proof of the intention of her Majesty's Government not to be ousted from its position in South Africa.'

Such were the grave and measured words with which the British pro-consul warned his countrymen of what was to come. He saw the storm cloud piling in the north, but even his eyes had not yet discerned how near and how terrible was the tempest.

Throughout the end of June and the early part of July much was hoped from the mediation of the heads of the Afrikander Bond, the political union of the Dutch Cape colonists. On the one hand, they were the kinsmen of the Boers; on the other, they were British subjects, and were enjoying the blessings of those liberal institutions which we were anxious to see extended to the Transvaal. 'Only treat our folk as we treat yours!' Our whole contention was compressed into that prayer. But nothing came of the mission, though a scheme endorsed by Mr. Hofmeyr and Mr. Herholdt, of the Bond, with Mr. Fischer of the Free State, was introduced into the Raad and applauded by Mr. Schreiner, the Africander Premier of Cape Colony. In its original form the provisions were obscure and complicated, the franchise varying from nine years to seven under different conditions. In debate, however, the terms were amended until the time was reduced to seven years, and the proposed representation of the Goldfields placed at five. The concession was not a great one, nor could the representation, five out of thirty-one, be considered a generous provision for half the adult male population; but the reduction of the years of residence was eagerly hailed in England as a sign that a compromise might be effected. A sigh of relief went up from the country. 'If,' said the Colonial Secretary, 'this report is confirmed, this important change in the proposals of President Kruger, coupled with previous amendments, leads Government to hope that the new law may prove to be the basis of a settlement on the lines laid down by Sir Alfred Milner in the Bloemfontein Conference.' He added that there were some vexatious conditions attached, but concluded, 'Her Majesty's Government feel assured that the President, having accepted the principle for which they have contended, will be prepared to reconsider any detail of his scheme which can be shown to be a possible hindrance to the full accomplishment of the object in view, and that he will not allow them to be nullified or reduced in value by any subsequent alterations of the law or acts of administration.' At the same time, the 'Times' declared the crisis to be at an end: 'If the Dutch statesmen of the Cape have induced their brethren in the Transvaal to carry such a Bill, they will have deserved the lasting gratitude, not only of their own countrymen and of the English colonists in South Africa, but of the British Empire and of the civilised world.' The reception of the idea that the crisis was at an end is surely a conclusive proof how little it was desired in England that that crisis should lead to war.

But this fair prospect was soon destined to be overcast. Questions of detail arose which, when closely examined, proved to be matters of very essential importance. The Uitlanders and British South Africans, who had experienced in the past how illusory the promises of the President might be, insisted upon guarantees. The seven years offered were two years more than that which Sir Alfred Milner had declared to be an irreducible minimum. The difference of two years would not have hindered their acceptance, even at the expense of some humiliation to our representative. But there were conditions which excited distrust when drawn up by so wily a diplomatist. One was that the alien who aspired to burghership had to produce a certificate of continuous registration for a certain time. But the law of registration had fallen into disuse in the Transvaal, and consequently this provision might render the whole Bill valueless. Since it was carefully retained, it was certainly meant for use. The door had been opened, but a stone was placed to block it. Again, the continued burghership of the new-comers was made to depend upon the resolution of the first Raad, so that should the mining members propose any measure of reform, not only their Bill but they also might be swept out of the house by a Boer majority. What could an Opposition do if a vote of the Government might at any moment unseat them all? It was clear that a measure which contained such provisions must be very carefully sifted before a British Government could accept it as a final settlement and a complete concession of justice to its subjects. On the other hand, it naturally felt loath to refuse those clauses which offered some prospect of an amelioration in their condition. It took the course, therefore, of suggesting that each Government should appoint delegates to form a joint commission which should inquire into the working of the proposed Bill before it was put into a final form. The proposal was submitted to the Raad on August 7, with the addition that when this was done Sir Alfred Milner was prepared to discuss anything else, including arbitration without the interference of foreign powers.

The suggestion of this joint commission has been criticised as an unwarrantable intrusion into the internal affairs of another country. But then the whole question from the beginning was about the internal affairs of another country, since there could be no rest in South Africa so long as one race tried to dominate the other. It is futile to suggest analogies, and to imagine what France would do if Germany were to interfere in a question of French franchise. Supposing that France contained nearly as many Germans as Frenchmen, and that they were ill-treated, Germany would interfere quickly enough and continue to do so until some fair *modus vivendi* was established. The fact is that the case of the Transvaal stands alone, that such a condition of things has never been known, and that no previous precedent can apply to it, save the general rule that white men who are heavily taxed must have some representation. Sentiment may incline to the smaller nation, but reason and justice are all on the side of Britain.

A long delay followed upon the proposal of the Secretary of the Colonies. No reply was forthcoming from Pretoria. But on all sides there came evidence that those preparations for war which had been quietly going on even before the Jameson Raid were now being hurriedly perfected. For so small a State enormous sums were being spent upon military equipment. Cases of rifles and boxes of cartridges streamed into the arsenal, not only from Delagoa Bay, but even, to the indignation of the English colonists, through Cape Town and Port Elizabeth. Huge packing-cases, marked 'Agricultural Instruments' and 'Mining Machinery,' arrived from Germany and France, to find their places in the forts of Johannesburg or Pretoria. As early as May the Orange Free State President, who was looked upon by the simple and trustful British as the honest broker who was about to arrange a peace, was writing to Grobler, the Transvaal official, claiming his share of the twenty-five million cartridges which had then been imported. This was the man who was posing as mediator between the two parties a fortnight later at Bloemfontein.

For three years the Transvaal had been arming to the teeth. So many modern magazine-rifles had been imported that there were enough to furnish five to every male burgher in the country. The importation of ammunition was on the same gigantic scale. For what were these formidable preparations? Evidently for a war with Great Britain and not for a defensive war. It is not in a defensive war that a State provides sufficient rifles to arm every man of Dutch blood in the whole of South Africa. No British reinforcements had been sent during the years that the Transvaal was obviously preparing for a struggle. In that one eloquent fact lies a complete proof as to which side forced on a war, and which side desired to avoid one. For three weeks and more, during which Mr. Kruger was silent, these preparations went on more energetically and more openly.

But beyond them, and of infinitely more importance, there was one fact which dominated the situation and retarded the crisis. A burgher cannot go to war without his horse, his horse cannot move without grass, grass will not come until after rain, and it was still some weeks before the rain would be due. Negotiations, then, must not be unduly hurried while the veldt was a bare russet-coloured dust-swept plain. Mr. Chamberlain and the British public waited week after week for an answer. But there was a limit to their patience, and it was reached on August 26, when the Colonial Secretary showed, with a plainness of speech which is as unusual as it is welcome in diplomacy, that the question could not be hung up forever. 'The sands are running down in the glass,' said he. 'If they run out we shall not hold ourselves limited by that which we have already offered, but, having taken the matter in hand, we will not let it go until we have secured conditions which once for all shall establish which is the paramount power in South Africa, and shall secure for our fellow-subjects there those equal rights and equal privileges which were promised them by President Kruger when the independence of the Transvaal was granted by the Queen, and which is the least that in justice ought to be accorded them.' Lord Salisbury, a short time before, had been equally emphatic: 'No one in this country wishes to disturb the conventions so long as it is recognised that while they guarantee the independence of the Transvaal on the one side, they guarantee equal political and civil rights for settlers of all nationalities upon the other. But these conventions are not like the laws of the Medes and the Persians. They are mortal, they can be destroyed...and once destroyed they can never be reconstructed in the same shape.' The long-enduring patience of Great Britain was beginning to show signs of giving way.

Pressure was in the meanwhile being put upon the old President and upon his advisers, if he can be said ever to have had any advisers, in order to induce him to accept the British offer of a joint committee of inquiry. Sir Henry de Villiers, representing the highest Africander opinion of the Cape, wrote strongly pleading the cause of peace, and urging Mr. Fischer of the Free State to endeavour to give a more friendly tone to the negotiations. 'Try to induce President Kruger to meet Mr. Chamberlain in a friendly way, and remove all the causes of unrest which have disturbed this unhappy country for so many years.' Similar advice came from Europe. The Dutch minister telegraphed as follows:

'*August 4, 1899.*—Communicate confidentially to the President that, having heard from the Transvaal Minister the English proposal of the International Commission, I recommend the President, in the interest of the country, not peremptorily to refuse that proposition.'

'*August 15, 1899.*—Please communicate confidentially to the President that the German Government entirely shares my opinion expressed in my despatch of August 4, not to refuse the English proposal. The German Government is, like myself, convinced that every approach to one of the Great Powers in this very critical moment will be without any results whatever, and very dangerous for the Republic.'

But neither his Africander brothers nor his friends abroad could turn the old man one inch from the road upon which he had set his foot. The fact is, that he knew well that his franchise proposals would not bear examination; that, in the words of an eminent lawyer, they 'might as well have been seventy years as seven,' so complicated and impossible were the conditions. For a long time he was silent, and when he at last spoke it was to open a new phase of the negotiations. His ammunition was not all to hand yet, his rifles had not all been distributed, the grass had not appeared upon the veldt. The game must be kept going for a couple of months. 'You are such past-masters in the art of gaining time!' said Mr. Labouchere to Mr. Montague White. The President proceeded to prove it.

His new suggestions were put forward on August 12. In them the Joint Commission was put aside, and the proposal was made that the Boer Government should accede to the franchise proposals of Sir Alfred Milner on condition that the British Government withdrew or dropped her claim to a suzerainty, agreed to arbitration by a British and South African tribunal, and promised never again to interfere in the internal affairs of the Republic. To this Great Britain answered that she would agree to such arbitration; that she hoped never again to have occasion to interfere for the protection of her own subjects, but that with the grant of the franchise all occasion for such interference would pass away; and, finally, that she would never consent to abandon her position as suzerain power. Mr. Chamberlain's despatch ended by reminding the Government of the Transvaal that there were other matters of dispute open between the two Governments apart from the franchise, and that it would be as well to have them settled at the same time. By these he meant such questions as the position of the native races and the treatment of Anglo-Indians.

For a moment there seemed now to be a fair prospect of peace. There was no very great gap between the two parties, and had the negotiations been really *bonâ fide* it seems incredible that it could not be bridged. But the Transvaal was secure now of the alliance of the Orange Free State; it believed that the Colony was ripe for rebellion; and it knew that with 60,000 cavalry and 100 guns it was infinitely the strongest military power in Africa. One cannot read the negotiations without being convinced that they were never meant to succeed, and the party which did not mean them to succeed was the party which prepared all the time for war. De Villiers, a friendly critic, says of the Transvaal Government: 'Throughout the negotiations they have always been wriggling to prevent a clear and precise decision.' Surely the sequel showed clearly enough why this was so. Their military hand was stronger than their political one, and it was with that that they desired to play the game. It would not do, therefore, to get the negotiations into such a stage that a peaceful solution should become inevitable. What was the use of all those rifles and cannon if the pen were after all to effect a compromise? 'The only thing that we are afraid of,' wrote young Blignant, 'is that Chamberlain with his admitted fitfulness of temper should cheat us out of our war and, consequently, the opportunity of annexing the Cape Colony and Natal, and forming the Republican United

States of South Africa'—a legitimate national ambition perhaps, but not compatible with *bonâ-fide* peaceful negotiations.

It was time, then, to give a less promising turn to the situation. On September 2 the answer of the Transvaal Government was returned. It was short and uncompromising. They withdrew their offer of the franchise. They reasserted the non-existence of the suzerainty. The negotiations were at a deadlock. It was difficult to see how they could be reopened. In view of the arming of the burghers, the small garrison of Natal had been taking up positions to cover the frontier. The Transvaal asked for an explanation of their presence. Sir Alfred Milner answered that they were guarding British interests, and preparing against contingencies. The roar of the fall was sounding loud and near.

On September 8 there was held a Cabinet Council—one of the most important in recent years. The military situation was pressing. The handful of troops in Africa could not be left at the mercy of the large and formidable force which the Boers could at any time hurl against them. On the other hand, it was very necessary not to appear to threaten or to appeal to force. For this reason reinforcements were sent upon such a scale as to make it evident that they were sent for defensive, and not for offensive, purposes. Five thousand men were sent from India to Natal, and the Cape garrisons were strengthened from England.

At the same time that they took these defensive measures, a message was sent to Pretoria, which even the opponents of the Government have acknowledged to be temperate, and offering the basis for a peaceful settlement. It begins by repudiating emphatically the claim of the Transvaal to be a sovereign international State in the same sense in which the

Orange Free State is one. Any proposal made conditional upon such an acknowledgment could not be entertained. The status of the Transvaal was settled by certain conventions agreed to by both Governments, and nothing had occurred to cause us to acquiesce in a radical change in it.

The British Government, however, was prepared to accept the five years' franchise as stated in the note of August 19, assuming at the same time that in the Raad each member might use his own language.

'Acceptance of these terms by the South African Republic would at once remove tension between the two Governments, and would in all probability render unnecessary any future intervention to secure redress for grievances which the Uitlanders themselves would be able to bring to the notice of the Executive Council and the Volksraad.

'Her Majesty's Government are increasingly impressed with the danger of further delay in relieving the strain which has already caused so much injury to the interests of South Africa, and they earnestly press for an immediate and definite reply to the present proposal. If it is acceded to they will be ready to make immediate arrangements ... to settle all details of the proposed tribunal of arbitration.... If, however, as they most anxiously hope will not be the case, the reply of the South African Republic should be negative or inconclusive, I am to state that Her Majesty's Government must reserve to themselves the right to reconsider the situation *de novo*, and to formulate their own proposals for a final settlement.'

This despatch was so moderate in form and so courteous in tone that press and politicians of every shade of opinion were united in approving it, and hoping for a corresponding reply which would relax the tension between the two nations. Mr. Morley, Mr. Leonard Courtney, the 'Daily Chronicle'—all the most strenuous opponents of the Government policy—were satisfied that it was a message of peace. But nothing at that time, save a complete and abject surrender upon the part of the British, could have satisfied the Boers, who had the most exaggerated ideas of their own military prowess and no very high opinion of our own. The continental conception of the British wolf and the Transvaal lamb would have raised a laugh in Pretoria, where the outcome of the war was looked upon as a foregone conclusion. The burghers were in no humour for concessions. They knew their own power, and they concluded with justice that they were for the time far the strongest military power in South Africa. 'We have beaten England before, but it is nothing to the licking that we shall give her now!' said one prominent citizen. 'Reitz seemed to treat the whole matter as a big joke,' remarked de Villiers. 'Is it really necessary for you to go,' said the Chief Justice of the Transvaal to an English clergyman. 'The war will be over in a fortnight. We shall take Kimberley and Mafeking and give the English such a beating in Natal that they will sue for peace.' Such were the extravagant ideas which caused them to push aside the olive-branch of peace.

On September 18 the official reply of the Boer Government to the message sent from the Cabinet Council was published in London. In manner it was unbending and unconciliatory; in substance, it was a complete rejection of all the British demands. It refused to recommend or propose to the Raad the five-years' franchise and the other provisions which had been defined as the minimum which the Home Government could accept as a fair measure of justice towards the Uitlanders. The suggestion that the debates of the Raad should be bilingual, as they are in the Cape Colony and in Canada, was absolutely waved aside. The British

Government had stated in their last despatch that if the reply should be negative or inconclusive they reserved to themselves the right to 'reconsider the situation *de novo*, and to formulate their own proposals for a final settlement.' The reply had been both negative and inconclusive, and on September 22 a council met to determine what the next message should be. It was short and firm, but so planned as not to shut the door upon peace. Its purport was that the British Government expressed deep regret at the rejection of the moderate proposals which had been submitted in their last despatch, and that now, in accordance with their promise, they would shortly put forward their own plans for a settlement. The message was not an ultimatum, but it foreshadowed an ultimatum in the future.

In the meantime, upon September 21, the Raad of the Orange Free State had met, and it became more and more evident that this republic, with whom we had no possible quarrel, but, on the contrary, for whom we had a great deal of friendship and admiration, intended to throw in its weight against Great Britain. Some time before, an offensive and defensive alliance had been concluded between the two States, which must, until the secret history of these events comes to be written, appear to have been a singularly rash and unprofitable bargain for the smaller one. She had nothing to fear from Great Britain, since she had been voluntarily turned into an independent republic by her, and had lived in peace with her for forty years. Her laws were as liberal as our own. But by this suicidal treaty she agreed to share the fortunes of a State which was deliberately courting war by its persistently unfriendly attitude, and whose reactionary and narrow legislation would, one might imagine, have alienated the sympathy of her progressive neighbour. The trend of events was seen clearly in the days of President Brand, who was a sane and experienced politician. 'President Brand,' says Paul Botha (himself a voortrekker and a Boer of the Boers), 'saw clearly what our policy ought to have been. He always avoided offending the Transvaal, but he loved the Orange Free State and its independence for its own sake and not as an appendage to the Transvaal. And in order to maintain its character he always strove for the friendship of England.

'President Brand realised that closer union with the turbulent and misguided Transvaal, led by Kruger's challenging policy, would inevitably result in a disastrous war with England.

'I [Paul Botha] felt this as strongly, and never ceased fighting against closer union. I remember once stating these arguments in the Volksraad, and wound up my speech by saying, "May Heaven grant that I am wrong in what I fear, because, if I am right, then woe, woe to the Orange Free State."'

It is evident that if the Free State rushed headlong to utter destruction it was not for want of wise voices which tried to guide her to some safer path. But there seems to have been a complete hallucination as to the comparative strength of the two opponents, and as to the probable future of South Africa. Under no possible future could the Free State be better off than it was already, a perfectly free and independent republic; and yet the country was carried away by race-prejudice spread broadcast from a subsidised press and an unchristian pulpit. 'When I come to think of the abuse the pulpit made of its influence,' says Paul Botha, 'I feel as if I cannot find words strong enough to express my indignation. God's word was prostituted. A religious people's religion was used to urge them to their destruction. A minister of God told me himself, with a wink, that he had to preach anti-English because otherwise he would lose favour with those in power.' Such were the influences which induced the Free State to make an insane treaty, compelling it to wantonly take up arms against a State which had never injured it and which bore it nothing but good will.

The tone of President Steyn at the meeting of the Raad, and the support which he received from the majority of his burghers, showed unmistakably that the two republics would act as one. In his opening speech Steyn declared uncompromisingly against the British contention, and declared that his State was bound to the Transvaal by everything which was near and dear. Among the obvious military precautions which could no longer be neglected by the British Government, was the sending of some small force to protect the long and exposed line of railway which lies just outside the Transvaal border from Kimberley to Rhodesia. Sir Alfred Milner communicated with President Steyn as to this movement of troops, pointing out that it was in no way directed against the Free State. Sir Alfred Milner added that the Imperial Government was still hopeful of a friendly settlement with the Transvaal, but if this hope were disappointed they looked to the Orange Free State to preserve strict neutrality and to prevent military intervention by any of its citizens. They undertook that in that case the integrity of the Free State frontier would be strictly preserved. Finally, he stated that there was absolutely no cause to disturb the good relations between the Free State and Great Britain, since we were animated by the most friendly intentions towards them. To this the President returned a somewhat ungracious answer, to the effect that he disapproved of our action towards the Transvaal, and that he regretted the movement of troops, which would be considered a menace by the burghers. A subsequent resolution of the Free State Raad, ending with the words, 'Come what may, the Free State will honestly and faithfully fulfil its obligations towards the Transvaal by virtue of the political alliance existing between the two republics,' showed how impossible it was that this country, formed by ourselves, and without a shadow of a cause of quarrel with us, could be saved from being drawn into the whirlpool.

In the meantime, military preparations were being made upon both sides, moderate in the case of the British and considerable in that of the Boers.

On August 15, at a time when the negotiations had already assumed a very serious phase, after the failure of the Bloemfontein Conference and the despatch of Sir Alfred Milner, the British forces in South Africa were absolutely and absurdly inadequate for the purpose of the defence of our own frontier. Surely such a fact must open the eyes of those who, in spite of all the evidence, persist that the war was forced on by the British. A statesman who forces on a war usually prepares for a war, and this is exactly what Mr. Kruger did and the British authorities did not. The overbearing suzerain power had at that date, scattered over a huge frontier, two cavalry regiments, three field batteries, and six and a half infantry battalions—say six thousand men. The innocent pastoral States could put in the field more than fifty thousand mounted riflemen, whose mobility doubled their numbers, and a most excellent artillery, including the heaviest guns which have ever been seen upon a battlefield. At this time it is most certain that the Boers could have made their way easily either to Durban or to Cape Town. The British force, condemned to act upon the defensive, could have been masked and afterwards destroyed, while the main body of the invaders would have encountered nothing but an irregular local resistance, which would have been neutralised by the apathy or hostility of the Dutch colonists. It is extraordinary that our authorities seem never to have contemplated the possibility of the Boers taking the initiative, or to have understood that in that case our belated reinforcements would certainly have had to land under the fire of the republican guns. They ran a great military risk by their inaction, but at least they made it clear to all who are not wilfully blind how far from the thoughts or wishes of the British Government it has always been that the matter should be decided by force.

In answer to the remonstrances of the Colonial Prime Minister the garrison of Natal was gradually increased, partly by troops from Europe, and partly by the despatch of 5,000 British troops from India. Their arrival late in September raised the number of troops in South Africa to 22,000, a force which was inadequate to a contest in the open field with the numerous, mobile, and gallant enemy to whom they were to be opposed, but which proved to be strong enough to stave off that overwhelming disaster which, with our fuller knowledge, we can now see to have been impending.

In the weeks which followed the despatch of the Cabinet message of September 8, the military situation had ceased to be desperate, but was still precarious. Twenty-two thousand regular troops were on the spot who might hope to be reinforced by some ten thousand Colonials, but these forces had to cover a great frontier, the attitude of Cape Colony was by no means whole-hearted and might become hostile, while the black population might conceivably throw in its weight against us. Only half the regulars could be spared to defend Natal, and no reinforcements could reach them in less than a month from the outbreak of hostilities. If Mr. Chamberlain was really playing a game of bluff, it must be confessed that he was bluffing from a very weak hand.

For purposes of comparison we may give some idea of the forces which Mr. Kruger and Mr. Steyn could put in the field. The general press estimate of the forces of the two republics varied from 25,000 to 35,000 men. Mr. J. B. Robinson, a personal friend of President Kruger's and a man who had spent much of his life among the Boers, considered the latter estimate to be too high. The calculation had no assured basis to start from. A very scattered and isolated population, among whom large families were the rule, is a most difficult thing to estimate. Some reckoned from the supposed natural increase during eighteen years, but the figure given at that date was itself an assumption. Others took their calculation from the number of voters in the last presidential election; but no one could tell how many abstentions there had been, and the fighting age is five years earlier than the voting age in the republics. We recognise now that all calculations were far below the true figure. It is probable, however, that the information of the British Intelligence Department was not far wrong. No branch of the British Service has come better out of a very severe ordeal than this one, and its report before the war is so accurate, alike in facts and in forecast, as to be quite prophetic.

According to this the fighting strength of the Transvaal alone was 32,000 men, and of the Orange Free State 22,000. With mercenaries and rebels from the colonies they would amount to 60,000, while a considerable rising of the Cape Dutch would bring them up to 100,000. Our actual male prisoners now amount to 42,000, and we can account for 10,000 casualties, so that, allowing another 10,000 for the burghers at large, the Boer force, excluding a great number of Cape rebels, would reach 62,000. Of the quality of this large force there is no need to speak. The men were brave, hardy, and fired with a strange religious enthusiasm. They were all of the seventeenth century, except their rifles. Mounted upon their hardy little ponies, they possessed a mobility which practically doubled their numbers and made it an impossibility ever to outflank them. As marksmen they are supreme. Add to this that they had the advantage of acting upon internal lines with shorter and safer communications, and one gathers how formidable a task lay before the soldiers of the Empire. When we turn from such an enumeration of their strength to contemplate the 12,000 men, split into two detachments, who awaited them in Natal, we may recognise that, far from bewailing our disasters, we should rather congratulate ourselves upon our escape from losing that great province which, situated as it is between Britain, India, and Australia, must be regarded as the very keystone of the imperial arch.

But again one must ask whether in the face of these figures it is still possible to maintain that Great Britain was deliberately attempting to overthrow by force the independence of the republics.

There was a lull in the political exchanges after the receipt of the Transvaal despatch of September 16, which rejected the British proposals of September 8. In Africa all hope or fear of peace had ended. The Raads had been dissolved and the old President's last words had been that war was certain, with a stern invocation of the Lord as the final arbiter. Britain was ready less obtrusively, but no less heartily, to refer the quarrel to the same dread judge.

On October 2 President Steyn informed Sir Alfred Milner that he had deemed it necessary to call out the Free State burghers—that is, to mobilise his forces. Sir A. Milner wrote regretting these preparations, and declaring that he did not yet despair of peace, for he was sure that any reasonable proposal would be favourably considered by her Majesty's Government. Steyn's reply was that there was no use in negotiating unless the stream of British reinforcements ceased coming into South Africa. As our forces were still in a great minority, it was impossible to stop the reinforcements, so the correspondence led to nothing. On October 7 the army reserves for the First Army Corps were called out in Great Britain, and other signs shown that it had been determined to send a considerable force to South Africa. Parliament was also summoned, that the formal national assent might be gained for those grave measures which were evidently pending.

It has been stated that it was the action of the British in calling out the reserves which caused the ultimatum from the Boers and so precipitated the war. Such a contention is absurd, for it puts the cart before the horse. The Transvaal commandos had mobilised upon September 27, and those of the Free State on October 2. The railways had been taken over, the exodus from Johannesburg had begun, and an actual act of war had been committed by the stopping of a train and the confiscation of the gold which was in it. The British action was subsequent to all this, and could not have been the cause of it. But no Government could see such portents and delay any longer to take those military preparations which were called for by the critical situation. As a matter of fact, the Boer ultimatum was prepared before the date of the calling out of the reserves, and was only delivered later because the final details for war were not quite ready.

It was on October 9 that the somewhat leisurely proceedings of the British Colonial Office were brought to a head by the arrival of an unexpected and audacious ultimatum from the Boer Government. In contests of wit, as of arms, it must be confessed that the laugh has up to now been usually upon the side of our simple and pastoral South African neighbours. The present instance was no exception to the rule. The document was very firm and explicit, but the terms in which it was drawn were so impossible that it was evidently framed with the deliberate purpose of forcing an immediate war. It demanded that the troops upon the borders of the republic should be instantly withdrawn, that all reinforcements which had arrived within the last year should leave South Africa, and that those who were now upon the sea should be sent back without being landed. Failing a satisfactory answer within forty-eight hours, 'The Transvaal Government will with great regret be compelled to regard the action of her Majesty's Government as a formal declaration of war, for the consequences of which it will not hold itself responsible.' The audacious message was received throughout the empire with a mixture of derision and anger. The answer was despatched next day through Sir Alfred Milner.

'*October 10.*—Her Majesty's Government have received with great regret the peremptory demands of the Government of the South African Republic, conveyed in your telegram of the 9th October. You will inform the Government of the South African Republic in reply that the conditions demanded by the Government of the South African Republic are such as her Majesty's Government deem it impossible to discuss.'

IV. SOME POINTS EXAMINED

Such is a general sketch of the trend of the negotiations and of the events which led up to the war. Under their different headings I will now examine in as short a space as possible the criticisms to which the British Government has been subjected. Various damaging theories and alternate lines of action have been suggested, each of which may be shortly discussed.

1. *That Mr. Chamberlain was personally concerned in the raid and that out of revenge for that failure, or because he was in the power of Mr. Rhodes, he forced on the war.*— The theory that Mr. Chamberlain was in the confidence of the raiders, has been already examined and shown to be untenable. That he knew that an insurrection might probably result from the despair of the Uitlanders is very probable. It was his business to know what was going on so far as he could, and there is no reason why his private sympathies, like those of every other Englishman, should not be with his own ill-used people. But that he contemplated an invasion of the Transvaal by a handful of policemen is absurd. If he did, why should he instantly take the strongest steps to render the invasion abortive? What could he possibly do to make things miscarry which he did not do? And if he were conscious of being in the power of Mr. Rhodes, how would he dare to oppose with such vigour that gentleman's pet scheme? The very facts and the very telegrams upon which critics rely to prove Mr. Chamberlain's complicity will really, when looked at with unprejudiced eyes, most clearly show his entire independence. Thus when Rhodes, or Harris in Rhodes's name, telegraphs, 'Inform Chamberlain that I shall get through all right if he will support me, but he must not send cable like he sent to the High Commissioner,' and again, 'Unless you can make Chamberlain instruct the High Commissioner to proceed at once to Johannesburg the whole position is lost,' is it not perfectly obvious that there has been no understanding of any sort, and that the conspirators are attempting to force the Colonial Secretary's hand? Again, critics make much of the fact that shortly before the raid Mr. Chamberlain sold to the Chartered Company the strip of land from which the raid started, and that he made a hard bargain, exacting as much as 200,000£. for it. Surely the perversion of an argument could hardly go further, for if Mr. Chamberlain were in their

confidence and in favour of their plan it is certain that he would have given them easy and not difficult terms for the land for which they asked. The supposition that Mr. Chamberlain was the tool of Rhodes in declaring war, presupposes that Mr. Chamberlain could impose his will without question upon a Cabinet which contained Lord Salisbury, Lord Lansdowne, Arthur Balfour, Hicks-Beach, and the other ministers. Such a supposition is too monstrous to discuss.

2. *That it is a capitalists' war, engineered by company promoters and Jews.*—After the Jameson Raid a large body of the public held this view, and it was this which to a great extent tied the hands of the Government, and stopped them from taking that strong line which might have prevented the accumulation of those huge armaments which could only be intended for use against ourselves. It took years to finally dissipate the idea, but how thoroughly it has been dissipated in the public mind is best shown by the patient fortitude with which our people have borne the long and weary struggle in which few families in the land have not lost either a friend or a relative. The complaisance of the British public towards capitalists goes no further than giving them their strict legal rights—and certainly does not extend to pouring out money and blood like water for their support. Such a supposition is absurd, nor can any reason be given why a body of high-minded and honourable British gentlemen like the Cabinet should sacrifice their country for the sake of a number of cosmopolitan financiers, most of whom are German Jews. The tax which will eventually be placed upon the Transvaal mining industry, in order to help to pay for the war, will in itself prove that the capitalists have no great voice in the councils of the nation. We know now that the leading capitalists in Johannesburg were the very men who most strenuously resisted an agitation which might lead to war. This seems natural enough when one

considers how much capitalists had at stake, and how much to lose by war. The agitation for the franchise and other rights was a *bonâ-fide* liberal agitation, started by poor men, employées and miners, who intended to live in the country, not in Park Lane. The capitalists were the very last to be drawn into it. When I say capitalists I mean the capitalists with British sympathies, for there is indeed much to be said in favour of the war being a capitalists' war, in that it was largely caused by the anti-British attitude and advice of the South African Netherlands Company, the Dynamite Monopoly, and other leeches which drained the country. To them a free and honest government meant ruin, and they strained every nerve, even to paying bogus English agitators, in order to hinder the cause of reform. Their attitude undoubtedly had something to do with stiffening the backs of the Boers and so preventing concessions.

3. *That Britain wanted the gold mines.*—No possible accusation is more popular or more widely believed upon the Continent, and yet none could be more ridiculous when it is examined. The gold mines are private companies, with shares held by private shareholders, German and French, as well as British. Whether the British or the Boer flag flew over the country would not alienate a single share from any holder, nor would the wealth of Britain be in any way greater. She will be the poorer by the vast expense of the war, and it is unlikely that more than one-third of this expenditure can be covered by taxation of the profits of the gold mines. Apart from this limited contribution towards the war, how is Britain the richer because her flag flies over the Rand? The Transvaal will be a self-governing colony, like all other British colonies, with its own finance minister, its own budget, its own taxes, even its own power of imposing duties upon British merchandise. They will pay a British governor 10,000£., and he will be expected to spend 15,000£. *We* know all this because it is part of our British

system, but it is not familiar to those nations who look upon colonies as sources of direct revenue to the mother country. It is the most general, and at the same time the most untenable, of all Continental comments upon the war. The second Transvaal war was the logical sequel of the first, and the first was fought before gold was discovered in the country.

4. *That it was a monarchy against a republic.*—This argument undoubtedly had weight with those true republics like the United States, France, and Switzerland, where people who were ignorant of the facts were led away by mere names. As a matter of fact Great Britain and the British colonies are among the most democratic communities in the world. They preserve, partly from sentiment, partly for political convenience, a hereditary chief, but the will of the people is decisive upon all questions, and every man by his vote helps to mould the destiny of the State. There is practically universal suffrage, and the highest offices of the State are within reach of any citizen who is competent to attain them. On the other hand, the Transvaal is an oligarchy, not a democracy, where half the inhabitants claim to be upon an entirely different footing from the other half. This rule represents the ascendency of one race over the other, such an ascendency as existed in Ireland in the eighteenth century. Technically the one country is a republic and the other a monarchy, but in truth the empire stood for liberty and the republic for tyranny, race ascendency, corruption, taxation without representation, and all that is most opposed to the broader conception of freedom.

5. *That it was a strong nation attacking a weak one.*—That appeal to sentiment and to the sporting instincts of the human race must always be a powerful one. But in this instance it is entirely misapplied. The preparation for war,

the ultimatum, the invasion, and the first shedding of blood, all came from the nation which the result has shown to be the weaker. The reason why this smaller nation attacked so audaciously was that they knew perfectly well that they were at the time far the stronger power in South Africa, and all their information led them to believe that they would continue to be so even when Britain had put forth all her strength. It certainly seemed that they were justified in this belief. The chief military critics of the Continent had declared that 100,000 men was the outside figure which Britain could place in the field. Against these they knew that without any rising of their kinsmen in the Cape they could place fifty or sixty thousand men, and their military history had unfortunately led them to believe that such a force of Boers, operating under their own conditions with their own horses in their own country, was far superior to this number of British soldiers. They knew how excellent was their artillery, and how complete their preparations. A dozen extracts could be given to show how confident they were of success, from Blignant's letter with his fears that Chamberlain would do them out of the war, to Esselen's boast that he would not wash until he reached the sea. What they did not foresee, and what put out their plans, was that indignant wave of public opinion throughout the British Empire which increased threefold—as it would, if necessary, have increased tenfold—the strength of the army and so enabled it to beat down the Boer resistance. When war was declared, and for a very long time afterwards, it was the Boers who were the strong power and the British who were the weak one, and any sympathy given on the other understanding was sympathy misapplied. From that time onwards the war had to take its course, and the British had no choice but to push it to its end.

6. *That the British refused to arbitrate.*—This has been repeated *ad nauseam*, but the allegation will not bear

investigation. There are some subjects which can be settled by arbitration, and all those Great Britain freely consented to treat in this fashion, before a tribunal which should be limited to Great Britain and South Africa. Such a tribunal would by no means be necessarily drawn from judges who were committed to one side or the other. There were many men whose moderation and discretion both sides would admit. Such a man, for example, was Rose Innes amongst the British, and de Villiers among those who had Africander sympathies. Both the Transvaal and the British Governments agreed that such a tribunal was competent, but they disagreed upon the point that the British Government desired to reserve some subjects from this arbitration.

The desire upon the part of Great Britain to exclude outsiders from the arbitration tribunal was due to the fact that to admit them was to give away the case before going into Court. The Transvaal claimed to be a sovereign international state. Great Britain denied it. If the Transvaal could appeal to arbitration as a peer among peers in a court of nations, she became *ipso facto* an international state. Therefore Great Britain refused such a court.

But why not refer all subjects to such a South African court as was finally accepted by both sides? The answer is that it is a monstrous hypocrisy to carry cases into an arbitration court, when you know beforehand that by their very nature they cannot possibly be settled by such a court. To quote Milner's words, 'It is, of course, absurd to suggest that the question whether the South African Republic does or does not treat British residents in that country with justice, and the British Government with the consideration and respect due to any friendly, not to say suzerain power, is a question capable of being referred to arbitration. You cannot arbitrate on broad questions of policy any more than on questions of national honour.' On this point of the limitation of arbitration the Transvaal leaders appear to have been as unanimous as the British, so that it is untrue to lay the blame of the restriction upon one side only. Mr. Reitz, in his scheme of arbitration formulated upon June 9, has the express clause 'That each side shall have the right to reserve and exclude points which appear to it to be too important to be submitted to arbitration.' To this the British Government agreed, making the further very great concession that an Orange Free Stater should not be regarded as a foreigner. The matter was in this state when the Transvaal sent its ultimatum. Up to the firing of the first shot the British Government still offered the only form of arbitration which was possible without giving away the question at issue. It was the Transvaal which, after agreeing to such a Court, turned suddenly to the arbitrament of the Mauser and the Creusot.

7. *That the war was to avenge Majuba.* — There can be no doubt that our defeat in this skirmish had left considerable heart-burnings which were not allayed by the subsequent attitude of the Boers and their assumption, testified to by Bryce and other friendly observers, that what we did after the action was due not to a magnanimous desire to repair a wrong but to craven fear. From the outset of the war there was a strong desire on the part of the soldiers to avenge Majuba, which was fully gratified when, upon the anniversary of that day, Cronje and his 4,000 brave companions had to raise the white flag. But that a desire to avenge Majuba swayed the policy of the country cannot be upheld in view of the fact that eighteen years had elapsed; that during that time the Boers had again and again broken the conventions by extending their boundaries; that three times matters were in such a position that war might have resulted and yet that peace was successfully maintained. War might very easily have been forced upon the Boers

during the years before they turned their country into an arsenal, when it would have been absolutely impossible for them to have sustained a long campaign. That it was not done and that the British Government remained patient until it received the outrageous ultimatum, is a proof that Majuba may have rankled in our memory but was not allowed to influence our policy.

8. *What proof is there that the Boers ever had any aggressive designs upon the British?*—It would be a misuse of terms to call the general Boer designs against the British a conspiracy, for it was openly advocated in the press, preached from the pulpit, and preached upon the platform, that the Dutch should predominate in South Africa, and that the portion of it which remained under the British flag should be absorbed by that which was outside it. So widespread and deep-seated was this ambition, that it was evident that Great Britain must, sooner or later, either yield to it or else sustain her position by force of arms. She was prepared to give Dutch citizens within her borders the vote, the power of making their own laws, complete religious and political freedom, and everything which their British comrades could have, without any distinction whatever; but when it came to hauling down the flag, it was certainly time that a stand should be made.

How this came about cannot be expressed more clearly than in the words of Paul Botha, who, as I have already said, was a voortrekker like Kruger himself, and a Boer of the Boers, save that he seems to have been a man with wider and more liberal views than his fellows. He was member for Kroonstadt in the Free State Raad.

'I am convinced,' he says, 'that Kruger's influence completely changed the character of the Afrikander Bond—an organisation which I believe Hofmeyr started at the Cape with the legitimate purpose of securing certain political privileges, but which, under Kruger's henchmen—Sauer, Merriman, Te Water, and others—raised unrest in the Cape Colony.

'This successful anti-British policy of Kruger created a number of imitators—Steyn, Fischer, Esselen, Smuts, and numerous other young educated Africanders of the Transvaal, Orange Free State, and the Cape Colony, who, misled by his successes, ambitiously hoped by the same means to raise themselves to the same pinnacle.

'Krugerism under them developed into a reign of terror. If you were anti- Kruger you were stigmatised as "Engelschgezind," and a traitor to your people, unworthy of a hearing. I have suffered bitterly from this taunt, especially under Steyn's *régime*. The more hostile you were to England the greater patriot you were accounted.

'This gang, which I wish to be clearly understood was spread over the whole of South Africa, the Transvaal, the Orange Free State, and the Cape Colony, used the Bond, the press, and the pulpit to further its schemes.

'Reitz, whom I believe to have been an honest enthusiast, set himself up as second sponsor to the Bond and voiced the doctrine of this gang: "Africa for the Africanders. Sweep the English into the sea." With an alluring cry like this, it will be readily understood how easy it was to inflame the imagination of the illiterate and uneducated Boer, and to work upon his vanity and prejudices. That pernicious rag, Carl Borckenhagen's "Bloemfontein Express," enormously contributed to spreading this doctrine in the Orange Free State. I myself firmly believe that the "Express" was subsidised by Kruger. It was no mystery to me from where Borckenhagen, a full-blooded German, got his ardent Free State patriotism.

'In the Transvaal this was done by the "Volksstem," written by a Hollander and subsidised by Kruger; by the "Rand Post," also written by a Hollander, also subsidised by Paul Kruger; and in the Cape Colony by the "Patriot," which was started by intriguers and rebels to their own Government, at the Paarl—a hot-bed of false Africanderism. "Ons Land" may be an honest paper, but by fostering impossible ideas it has done us incalculable harm. It grieves me to think that my poor people, through want of education, had to swallow this poison undiluted.

'Is it possible to imagine that Steyn, Fischer, and the other educated men of the Free State did not know that, following Kruger's hostile policy of eliminating the preponderating Power in South Africa, meant that that Power would be forced either to fight in self-preservation or to disappear ignominiously? For I maintain that there were only two courses open to England in answer to Kruger's challenging policy—to fight or to retire from South Africa. It was only possible for men suffering from tremendously swollen heads, such as our leaders were suffering from, not to see the obvious or to doubt the issue.'

So much for a Boer's straightforward account of the forces at work, and the influences which were at the back of those forces. It sums the situation up tersely, but the situation itself was evident and dominated Cape politics. The ambitions of Africanderdom were discussed in the broad light of day in the editorial, in the sermon, in the speech, though the details by which those ambitions were to be carried out were only whispered on the Dutch stoeps.

Here are the opinions of Reitz, the man who more than all others, save his master, has the blood of the fallen upon his conscience. It is taken from the 'Reminiscences' of Mr.

Theophilus Schreiner, the brother of the ex-Prime Minister of the Cape:

'I met Mr. Reitz, then a judge of the Orange Free State, in Bloemfontein between seventeen and eighteen years ago, shortly after the retrocession of the Transvaal, and when he was busy establishing the Afrikander Bond. It must be patent to everyone that at that time, at all events, England and its Government had no intention of taking away the independence of the Transvaal, for she had just "magnanimously" granted the same; no intention of making war on the republics, for she had just made peace; no intention to seize the Rand gold fields, for they were not yet discovered. At that time, then, I met Mr. Reitz, and he did his best to get me to become a member of his Afrikander Bond, but, after studying its constitution and programme, I refused to do so, whereupon the following colloquy in substance took place between us, which has been indelibly imprinted on my mind ever since:

'*Reitz*: Why do you refuse? Is the object of getting the people to take an interest in political matters not a good one?

'*Myself*: Yes, it is; but I seem to see plainly here between the lines of this constitution much more ultimately aimed at than that.

'*Reitz*: What?

'*Myself*: I see quite clearly that the ultimate object aimed at is the overthrow of the British power and the expulsion of the British flag from South Africa.

'*Reitz (with his pleasant conscious smile, as of one whose secret thought and purpose had been discovered, and who*

was not altogether displeased that such was the case):
Well, what if it is so?

'*Myself*: You don't suppose, do you, that that flag is going to disappear from South Africa without a tremendous struggle and fight?

'*Reitz (with the same pleasant self-conscious, self-satisfied, and yet semi-apologetic smile):* Well, I suppose not; but even so, what of that?

'*Myself*: Only this, that when that struggle takes place you and I will be on opposite sides; and what is more, the God who was on the side of the Transvaal in the late war, because it had right on its side, will be on the side of England, because He must view with abhorrence any plotting and scheming to overthrow her power and position in South Africa, which have been ordained by Him.

'*Reitz*: We'll see.

'Thus the conversation ended, but during the seventeen years that have elapsed I have watched the propaganda for the overthrow of British power in South Africa being ceaselessly spread by every possible means—the press, the pulpit, the platform, the schools, the colleges, the Legislature—until it has culminated in the present war, of which Mr. Reitz and his co-workers are the origin and the cause. Believe me, the day on which F. W. Reitz sat down to pen his ultimatum to Great Britain was the proudest and happiest moment of his life, and one which had for long years been looked forward to by him with eager longing and expectation.'

Compare with these utterances of a Dutch politician of the Cape, and of a Dutch politician of the Orange Free State, the following passage from a speech delivered by Kruger at

Bloemfontein in the year 1887, long before Jameson raids or franchise agitations:

'I think it too soon to speak of a United South Africa under one flag. Which flag was it to be? The Queen of England would object to having her flag hauled down, and we, the burghers of the Transvaal, object to hauling ours down. What is to be done? We are now small and of little importance, but we are growing, and are preparing the way to take our place among the great nations of the world.'

'The dream of our life,' said another, 'is a union of the States of South Africa, and this has to come from within, not from without. When that is accomplished, South Africa will be great.'

Always the same theory from all quarters of Dutch thought, to be followed by many signs that the idea was being prepared for in practice. I repeat, that the fairest and most unbiased historian cannot dismiss the movement as a myth.

And to this one may retort, Why should they not do so? Why should they not have their own views as to the future of South Africa? Why should they not endeavour to have one universal flag and one common speech? Why should they not win over our colonists, if they can, and push us into the sea? I see no reason why they should not. Let them try if they will. And let us try to prevent them. But let us have an end of talk about British aggression, of capitalist designs upon the gold fields, of the wrongs of a pastoral people, and all the other veils which have been used to cover the issue. Let those who talk about British designs upon the republics turn their attention for a moment to the evidence which there is for republican designs upon the colonies. Let them reflect that in the British system all white men are equal, and that in the Boer one race has persecuted the other; and let them consider under which the truest freedom lies, which stands for universal liberty, and which for reaction and racial hatred. Let them ponder and answer all this before they determine where their sympathies lie.

Long before the war, when the British public and the British Government also had every confidence that the solution would be found in peace, every burgher had been provided with his rifle, his ammunition, and his instructions as to the part which he was to play in that war which they looked upon as certain. A huge conspiracy as to the future, which might be verbally discussed but which must not be written, seems to have prevailed among the farmers. Curious evidence of it came into my own hands in this fashion. After a small action at which I was present I entered a deserted Boer farmhouse which had been part of the enemy's position, and, desiring to carry away some souvenir which should be of no value, I took some papers which appeared to be children's writing-exercises. They were so, but among them were one or two letters, one of which I append in all its frankness and simplicity. The date is some fourteen weeks *before*the declaration of war, when the British were anxious for and confident in a peaceful solution:

'Paradÿs, June 25, 1899.

'MY DEAR HENRY, I taking my pen up to write you these few lines. That we all are in good health, hoping to hear the same from you all. And the letter of the 18th is handed to me. And I feel very much obliged that I hear you are all in good health.... Here by us are the fields very dry, and the dams just by dry also. *Dear Henry, the war are by us very much. How is it there by you. News is very scarce to write, but much to speak by ourselves.* I must now close with my letter because I see that you will be tired out to read it. With best love to you and your family so I remain your faithfully friend,

'PIETER WIESE.'

Here is, in itself, as it seems to me, evidence of that great conspiracy, not of ambitions (for there was no reason why they should not be openly discussed), but of weapons and of dates for using them, which was going on all the time behind that cloud of suspicious negotiations with which the Boer Governments veiled their resolution to attack the British. A small straw, no doubt, but the result has shown how deep and dangerous was the current which it indicates. Here is a letter from one of the Snymans to his brother at a later period, but still a month before the war. He is talking of Kruger:

'The old chap was nearly raving about it, and said that the burghers wanted to tie his hands, and so, brother, the thing is simply war and nothing else. He said we had gone too far, and help from overseas was positively promised, only unanimity of opinion must reign here or we could neither expect nor obtain assistance. Brother, the old man and his Hollander dogs talk very easily about the thing; but what shall we do, because if one speaks against it one is simply a rebel? So I remain dumb.

'On the stoep it is nothing but war, but in the Raad everything is peace and Queen. Those are the politics they talk. I have nothing more to say here, but I can tell you a good deal. Brother, old Reitz says Chamberlain will have a great surprise one of these days, and the burghers must sleep with one eye open.

'It is rumoured here that our military officers work day and night to send old Victoria an ultimatum before she is ready.'

'On the stoep it is nothing but war, but in the Raad everything is peace.' No wonder the British overtures were in vain.

V. THE NEGOTIATIONS FOR PEACE

This is not an attempt to write the history of the war, which I have done elsewhere, but only to touch upon those various points upon which attempts have been made to mislead continental and American opinion. I will endeavour to treat each of these subjects in turn, not in the spirit of a lawyer preparing a brief, but with an honest endeavour to depict the matter as it is, even when I venture to differ from the action either of the British Government or of the generals in the field. In this chapter I will deal with the question of making peace, and examine how far the British are to blame for not having brought those negotiations which have twice been opened to a successful conclusion.

The outset of the war saw the Boers aggressive and victorious. They flocked into British territory, drove the small forces opposed to them into entrenched positions, and held them there at Ladysmith, Kimberley, and Mafeking. At the same time they drove back at Colenso and at Magersfontein the forces which were sent to relieve these places. During this long period of their predominance from October 1899 to February 1900, there was no word of peace. On the contrary, every yard of British territory which was occupied was instantly annexed either by the Transvaal or by the Orange Free State. This is admitted and beyond dispute. What becomes then of the theory of a defensive war, and what can they urge against the justice which awarded the same fate to the land of the Boers when it in turn was occupied by us? The Boers did not use their temporary victory in any moderate spirit. At the end of January 1900, Dr. Leyds, while on his visit to Berlin, said:

'I believe that England will have to give us back a good part of the territory formerly snatched away from us.... The

Boers will probably demand the cession of the strip of coast between Durban and Delagoa Bay, with the harbours of Lucia and Kosi. The Orange Free State and the Transvaal are to be united and to form one State, together with parts of Natal and the northern districts of Cape Colony.'—(*Daily News* Berlin correspondent, February 1, March 16, 1900.)

They were to go to the sea, and nothing but going to the sea would satisfy them. The war would end when their flag flew over Cape Town. But there came a turn of the tide. The resistance of the garrisons, the tenacity of the relieving forces, and the genius of Lord Roberts altered the whole situation. The Boers were driven back to the first of their capitals. Then for the first time there came from them those proposals for peace, which were never heard when the game was going in their favour. Here is President Kruger's telegram:

'THE PRESIDENTS OF THE ORANGE FREE STATE AND OF THE SOUTH AFRICAN REPUBLIC TO THE MARQUESS OF SALISBURY.

'Bloemfontein: March 5, 1900.

'The blood and the tears of the thousands who have suffered by this war, and the prospect of all the moral and economic ruin with which South Africa is now threatened, make it necessary for both belligerents to ask themselves dispassionately, and as in the sight of the Triune God, for what they are fighting, and whether the aim of each justifies all this appalling misery and devastation.

'With this object, and in view of the assertions of various British statesmen to the effect that this war was begun and is being carried on with the set purpose of undermining Her Majesty's authority in South Africa, and of setting up an Administration over all South Africa independent of Her

Majesty's Government, we consider it our duty solemnly to declare that this war was undertaken solely as a defensive measure to safeguard the threatened independence of the South African Republic, and is only continued in order to secure and safeguard the incontestable independence of both Republics as Sovereign International States, and to obtain the assurance that those of Her Majesty's subjects who have taken part with us in this war shall suffer no harm whatsoever in person or property.

'On these conditions, but on these conditions alone, are we now, as in the past, desirous of seeing peace re-established in South Africa, and of putting an end to the evils now reigning over South Africa; while, if Her Majesty's Government is determined to destroy the independence of the Republics, there is nothing left to us and to our people but to persevere to the end in the course already begun, in spite of the overwhelming pre-eminence of the British Empire, confident that that God who lighted the unextinguishable fire of the love of freedom in the hearts of ourselves and of our fathers will not forsake us, but will accomplish His work in us and in our descendants.

'We hesitated to make this declaration earlier to Your Excellency, as we feared that as long as the advantage was always on our side, and as long as our forces held defensive positions far in Her Majesty's colonies, such a declaration might hurt the feelings of honour of the British people; but now that the prestige of the British Empire may be considered to be assured by the capture of one of our forces by Her Majesty's troops, and that we are thereby forced to evacuate other positions which our forces had occupied, that difficulty is over, and we can no longer hesitate clearly to inform your Government and people in the sight of the whole civilised world why we are fighting, and on what conditions we are ready to restore peace.'

Here is Lord Salisbury's reply:

'Foreign Office: March 11, 1900.

'I have the honour to acknowledge Your Honours' telegram dated the 5th of March from Bloemfontein, of which the purport is principally to demand that Her Majesty's Government shall recognise the "incontestable independence" of the South African Republic and Orange Free State "as Sovereign International States," and to offer, on those terms, to bring the war to a conclusion.

'In the beginning of October last peace existed between Her Majesty and the two Republics under the Conventions which then were in existence. A discussion had been proceeding for some months between Her Majesty's Government and the South African Republic, of which the object was to obtain redress for certain very serious grievances under which British residents in the South African Republic were suffering. In the course of those negotiations the South African Republic had, to the knowledge of Her Majesty's Government, made considerable armaments, and the latter had, consequently, taken steps to provide corresponding reinforcements to the British garrisons of Cape Town and Natal. No infringement of the rights guaranteed by the Conventions had up to that point taken place on the British side. Suddenly, at two days' notice, the South African Republic, after issuing an insulting ultimatum, declared war upon Her Majesty, and the Orange Free State, with whom there had not even been any discussion, took a similar step. Her Majesty's dominions were immediately invaded by the two Republics, siege was laid to three towns within the British frontier, a large portion of the two colonies was overrun, with great destruction to property and life, and the Republics claimed to treat the inhabitants of extensive portions of Her

Majesty's dominions as if those dominions had been annexed to one or other of them. In anticipation of these operations, the South African Republic had been accumulating for many years past military stores on an enormous scale, which by their character could only have been intended for use against Great Britain.

'Your Honours make some observations of a negative character upon the object with which these preparations were made. I do not think it necessary to discuss the question you have raised. But the result of these preparations, carried on with great secrecy, has been that the British Empire has been compelled to confront an invasion which has entailed upon the Empire a costly war and the loss of thousands of precious lives. This great calamity has been the penalty which Great Britain has suffered for having in recent years acquiesced in the existence of the two Republics.

'In view of the use to which the two Republics have put the position which was given to them, and the calamities which their unprovoked attack has inflicted upon Her Majesty's dominions, Her Majesty's Government can only answer Your Honours' telegram by saying that they are not prepared to assent to the independence either of the South African Republic or of the Orange Free State.'

Is there any sane man of any nation who can contend that a British statesman could possibly have taken any other view? From the firing of the first shot the irresistible logic of events showed that either the Republics must dominate Africa or they must cease to exist. For the sparing of the Orange Free State there might, I think, be a fair argument, but they had put themselves out of court by annexing every foot of British territory which they could lay their hands upon. For the sparing of the Transvaal there could be no possible reason. Had that State been reconstituted we should instantly have been faced once more with the Franchise question, the Uitlander question, the corrupt oligarchy, the anti-British conspiracy, and everything which we had spent so much blood and money to set right. The desperate situation from which the British power was only just emerging was so fresh in our minds that we could not feel justified in leaving the possibility—indeed the certainty—of its recurrence to our children. Remember, you who judge us, that we had done all this before. Once before within our own memories we had patched up an inconclusive peace, and left these people the power to hurt us. And what had come of it? Eternal trouble ending in a great war which strained the resources of the Empire. Could we be asked to do the same again? Would any nation on earth have done the same again? From the day of the signing of peace we should know that we had an implacable and formidable foe to the north of us, nursing his wrath and preparing his strength for the day when he might strike us at an advantage. Our colonies would lie ever in the shadow of its menace. Who can blame us for deciding that the job should be done now in such a way that it should never, so far as we could help it, need to be done once more?

Such was the end of the first negotiations for peace. The war was resumed, and in time the second capital of the Boers was taken and President Kruger withdrew to Europe, leaving South Africa in the welter to which he had reduced it. Then, for the second time, negotiations for peace were opened on the initiative of General Botha, which led to a meeting upon February 28, 1901, between Kitchener and Botha. Kitchener had already explained that for the reasons given above the restoration of independence was impossible, and the negotiations were carried through on that understanding. Here is Lord Kitchener's own account of the interview and of the points at issue:

[*Telegram.*] 'Pretoria: March 1, 1901, 2.20 P.M.

'*28th February.*—I have had a long interview with Botha, who showed very good feeling and seemed anxious to bring about peace. He asked for information on a number of subjects which he said that he should submit to his Government and people, and if they agreed he should visit Orange River Colony and get them to agree. They should all then hand in their arms and finish the war. He told me that they could go on for some time, and that he was not sure of being able to bring about peace without independence. He tried very hard for some kind of independence, but I declined to discuss such a point, and said that a modified form of independence would be most dangerous and likely to lead to war in the future. Subject was then dropped, and—

'Firstly. — The nature of future government of Colonies asked about. He wanted more details than were given by Colonial Secretary, and I said that, subject to correction from home, I understood that when hostilities ceased military guard would be replaced by Crown Colony administration, consisting of nominated Executive, with elected assembly to advise administration, to be followed after a period by representative government. He would have liked representative government at once, but seemed satisfied with above.

'Secondly. — Whether a Boer would be able to have a rifle to protect him from native? I said I thought he would be by a licence and on registration.

'Thirdly. — He asked whether Dutch language would be allowed? I said that English and Dutch would, I thought, have equal rights. He expressed hope that officials dealing with farmers would know Dutch.

'Fourthly. — The Kaffir question. This turned at once on franchise of Kaffirs, and a solution seemed to be that franchise should not be given to Kaffirs until after representative government was granted to Colonies. Orange Free State laws for Kaffirs were considered good.

'Fifthly. — That Dutch Church property should remain untouched.

'Sixthly. — Public trusts and orphan funds to be left intact. He asked whether British Government, in taking over the assets of Republics, would also take over legal debts. This he made rather a strong point of, and he intended it to include debts legally contracted since the war began. He referred to notes issued amounting to less than a million.

'Seventhly. — He asked if any war tax would be imposed on farmers? I said I thought not.

'Eighthly. — When would prisoners of war return?

'Ninthly. — He referred to pecuniary assistance to repair burnt farms, and enable farmers to start afresh. I said I thought some assistance would be given.

'Tenthly. — Amnesty to all at end of war. We spoke of Colonials who joined Republics, and he seemed not adverse to their being disfranchised.

'I arranged with him that I should write and let him know the view of the Government on these points. All I said during the interview was qualified by being subject to confirmation from home. He was anxious to get an answer soon.'

There followed some correspondence between Lord Kitchener, Sir Alfred Milner, and Mr. Chamberlain upon the exact terms which could be given to Botha. They ended in the following offer, which was submitted to him upon March 7. That, in consideration of a complete military surrender,

'1. There should be a complete amnesty for all *bonâ fide* acts of war for all burghers of the Republics. In the case of Colonial rebels, if they returned to their Colonies some inquiry must be held on their conduct.

'2. All prisoners to be at once sent back.

'3. Crown Colony government to be given as soon as possible; this in turn to change to representative government, as in all other free British possessions. The courts of law to be independent of the government.

'4. The Dutch and English languages to be put upon an equality.

'5. That the Government should help to replace the farmers on their farms, to restore their buildings, should pledge itself not to specially tax them, and should pay as an act of grace one million pounds to meet the debt incurred by the Republican governments to their own people during the war.

'6. That the burghers be allowed sporting fire-arms.

'7. That the Kaffirs should have the protection of the law, but should not have the vote.

'In conclusion,' says Lord Kitchener, 'I must inform your honour that if the terms are not accepted after a reasonable delay for consideration, they must be regarded as cancelled.'

But the wise and chivalrous Botha was overruled by the men around him, many of whom had little to lose by a continuance of the struggle. It was evident that he did not himself consider independence vital, since he had gravely discussed terms which were based upon loss of independence. But other influences had been brought to bear upon him, and this was his reply—a reply which has already cost the lives of so many of each side:

'I have the honour to acknowledge receipt of Your Excellency's letter stating what steps Your Excellency's Government is prepared to take in the event of a general and total cessation of hostilities. I have advised my Government of Your Excellency's said letter; but, after the mutual exchange of views at our interview at Middelburg on 28th February last, it will certainly not surprise Your Excellency to know that I do not feel disposed to recommend that the terms of the said letter shall have the earnest consideration of my Government. I may add also that my Government and my chief officers here entirely agree to my views.'

It will be observed that in this reply Botha bases his refusal upon his own views as expressed in the original interview with Kitchener; and we have his own authority, therefore, to show that they were not determined by any changes which Chamberlain may have made in the terms—a favourite charge of that gentleman's enemies.

It is impossible to say how, short of independence, Great Britain could have improved upon these terms, and it has already been shown that to offer independence would mean having to fight the war over again. It has been suggested that Great Britain might have offered a definite date upon which representative institutions should come in force, but such a promise must be disingenuous, for it must evidently depend not upon a date, but upon the state of the country. The offers of loans to the farmers towards the stocking and rebuilding the farms were surely generous to our defeated foes, and, indeed, it is clear now that in some respects our generosity went too far, and that the interests of the Empire would have suffered severely had these terms been accepted. To have given more would certainly seem not to have offered peace, but to have implored it.

Whatever the final terms of peace may prove to be, it is to be earnestly hoped that 40,000 male prisoners will not be returned, as a matter of right, without any guarantee for their future conduct. It is also much to be desired that the bastard taal language, which has no literature and is almost as unintelligible to a Hollander as to an Englishman, will cease to be officially recognised. These two omissions may repay in the long run for weary months of extra war since, upon Botha's refusal, the British Government withdrew these terms and the hand moved onwards upon the dial of fate, never to turn back.

De Wet had said in reference to Kitchener's terms of peace, 'What is the use of examining all the points, as the only object for which we are fighting is our independence and our national existence?' It is evident, however, that Botha did not consider this an absolute bar to renewing the negotiations, for upon May 10, two months later, he wrote the following letter to Lord Kitchener:

'Commandant-General's Camp, May 10, 1901.

'EXCELLENCY, — As I have already assured Your Excellency I am very desirous of terminating this war, and its sad consequences. It is, however, necessary, in order to comply with the "Grondwet" of this Republic and otherwise, that, before any steps are taken in that direction, the condition of our country and our cause be brought to the notice of His Honour, State President Kruger, in Europe; and I therefore wish to send two persons to him in order to acquaint him fully with that condition.

'As speed in this matter is of great consequence to both contending parties, and as such despatch without Your Excellency's assistance would take a considerable time, I should like to hear from Your Excellency whether Your Excellency is prepared to assist me in expediting this matter by allowing such person or persons to journey there and back unhindered, if necessary by the traffic medium within Your Excellency's control. — I have, &c.,

'LOUIS BOTHA, Commandant-General.'

To this Kitchener answered:

'Army Headquarters, South Africa, Pretoria, May 16, 1901.

'YOUR HONOUR, — I have the honour to acknowledge the receipt of Your Honour's letter of 10th instant, and, in reply, beg to state that I can only deal with you and your superior officers in the field in regard to the cessation of hostilities, and that I do not recognise the official status of any other persons in the late Republics of the Orange River and Transvaal.

'If, however, Your Honour desires, with the object of bringing hostilities to a close, to consult with any person in Europe, I will forward any telegram Your Honour desires on the subject, and let you have the reply. Should, however, Your Honour still desire to send messengers, and will inform me of their names and status, I will refer the matter to His Majesty's Government for decision. — I have, &c.,

'KITCHENER, General,

'Commanding-in-Chief, British Troops, South Africa.'

At this period, the second week of May, the Boer cause was in very low water, as on the same date we have Botha reopening negotiations which he had declared to be definitely closed, and Reitz (the man who used to regard the whole matter as a great joke) writing a despairing letter to Steyn to the effect that the game was up and that it was time to take the last final step. A reply was received from Kruger encouraging the Boers to continue their hopeless and fatal resistance. His reply was to the effect that there were still great hopes of a successful issue of the war, and that he had taken steps to make proper provision for the Boer prisoners and for the refugee women. These steps, and very efficient ones, too, were to leave them to the generosity of that Government which he was so fond of reviling. There are signs that something else had occurred to give them fresh hope and also fresh material supplies. It looks, upon the face of it, as if, about that time, large supplies of rifles, ammunition, and possibly recruits must have reached them from some quarter, either from German Damaraland or the Portuguese coast. At any rate there has been so much ammunition used since, that either Reitz must have been raving or else large supplies have reached the Boers from some unknown source.

So much for the official attempts at peace.

They have been given in some detail in order to prove how false it is *that the British Government has insisted upon an unconditional surrender*. Far from this being so, the terms offered by the British Government have been so generous that they have aroused the strongest distrust and criticism in this country, where they have seemed to be surrendering by the pen all that had been won by the sword. Nothing has been refused the enemy, save only independence, and that can never be given, if the war has to continue until the last Boer is deported out of Africa.

It is only necessary to refer briefly to the unofficial Boer attempts at peace. A considerable body of the Boers, including many men of influence and of intelligence, were disposed to accept the British flag and to settle down in peace. The leaders of this party were the brave Piet de Wet, brother of Christian, Paul Botha of Kroonstad, Fraser of Bloemfontein, and others. Piet de Wet, who had fought against us as hard as any man, wrote to his brother: 'Which is better, for the Republics to continue the struggle and run the risk of total ruin as a nation, or to submit? Could we for a moment think of taking back the country, if it were offered to us, with thousands of people to be supported by a Government which has not a farthing? Put passionate feeling aside for a moment and use common-sense, and you will then agree with me that the best thing for the people and the country is to give in, to be loyal to the new Government, and to get responsible government.' Such were the sentiments of many of the best of the burghers, and they endeavoured to persuade their fellows. Both in the Transvaal and in the Free State, Peace Committees were formed among the burghers, who sent deputies to lay the facts of the situation before their brethren on commando. The results were tragic. Two of the envoys, Morgendaal and de Koch, were shot in cold blood, the former having been first beaten. Several of the others were beaten, and all were ill-used.

This severity did not, however, stop the movement, but gave it a fiercer turn. The burghers who were in favour of peace, finding it useless to argue with their fellow-countrymen and knowing that their country was being hopelessly ruined by the insensate resistance, took the extreme course at last of bearing arms against them. There are at present three strong commandos of burghers fighting upon the British side, commanded by three Boer Generals—Marais, Celliers, and the younger Cronje, all of whom had made their names in fighting against us. This fact alone goes far to dispel those stories of British barbarity with which I shall presently deal.

They are believed in by political fanatics in England and by dupes abroad, but the answer which many of the Boers upon the spot make to them is to enlist and fight under the British flag. They are in the best position for knowing the truth, and how can they show in a stronger way what they believe that truth to be?

VI. THE FARM-BURNING

In the official correspondence which is published between the Boer and British leaders in South Africa may very clearly be traced the way in which this practice came to assume proportions which shocked public opinion. It must be admitted that the results have not justified it, and that, putting all moral questions apart, a burned-out family is the last which is likely to settle down, as we hope that the Boers may eventually settle down, as contented British citizens. On the other hand, when a nation adopts guerilla tactics it deliberately courts those sufferings to the whole country which such tactics invariably entail. They have been the same in all wars and at all times. The army which is stung by guerillas, strikes round it furiously and occasionally indiscriminately. An army which is continually sniped and harassed becomes embittered, and a General feels called upon to take those harsher measures which precedent and experience suggest. That such measures have not been pushed to an extreme by the British authorities is shown by the fact that the captured guerilla has been made a prisoner of war—unlike his prototype, the *franc-tireur*. The general question of guerillas may be discussed later. At present we will confine our attention to the burning of farms.

The first protest from the Boer side is dated February 3, 1900. In it the two Presidents accuse the British troops 'of burning and blowing up with dynamite the farmhouses, and of the devastation of farms.' The document also includes an accusation of having used armed natives against the Boers.

Lord Roberts replied upon February 5 to the effect that stringent instructions had been given to the British troops to respect private property. 'All wanton destruction or injury to peaceful inhabitants is contrary to British practice and tradition, and will, if necessary, be rigorously repressed by me.' He added that it was an untrue statement that natives had ever been encouraged by British officers to commit depredations. The charge, which has been the subject of many effective cartoons upon the Continent, is as absurd as most of the other works of the same artists. Why should the State which refused the aid of its own highly trained Indian army of 150,000 men, avail itself of that of savages? Lord Roberts denied the assertion with befitting warmth, and it is not again repeated in the course of the despatches.

Lord Roberts in this document was not content with denying the Boer allegations, but carried the war into the enemy's country:

'I regret to say that it is the Republican forces which have in some cases been guilty of carrying on the war in a manner not in accordance with civilised usage. I refer especially to the expulsion of loyal subjects of Her Majesty from their homes in the invaded districts of this Colony, because they refused to be commandeered by the invader. It is barbarous to attempt to force men to take sides against their own Sovereign and country by threats of spoliation and expulsion. Men, women, and children have had to leave their homes owing to such compulsion, and many of those who were formerly in comfortable circumstances are now being maintained by charity.'

He adds: 'I beg to call your Honours' attention to the wanton destruction of property by the Boer forces in Natal. They not only have helped themselves freely to the cattle and other property of farmers without payment, but they have utterly wrecked the contents of many farmhouses. As an instance I would specify Mr. Theodore Wood's farm "Longwood" near Springfield. I point out how very different is the conduct of the British troops. It is reported to me from Modder River that farms within the actual area of the British Camp have never even been entered, the occupants are unmolested, and their houses, gardens, and crops remain absolutely untouched.'

On March 26 Lord Roberts's Proclamation spoke with no uncertain voice upon the subject of private property. It says:

'The following Proclamation, issued by me in the name of Her Majesty's Government on the 26th March, begins: Notice is hereby given that all persons who within the territories of the South African Republic or Orange Free State shall authorise or be guilty of the wanton destruction or damage or the counselling, aiding, or assisting in the wanton destruction or damage of public or private property, such destruction or damage not being justified by the usages and customs of civilised warfare, will be held responsible in their persons and property for all such wanton destruction and damage.'

This was during the period of the halt at Bloemfontein. I can well remember that then and for long afterwards the consideration which was shown upon this point seemed to those who were at the spot to be exaggerated and absurd. I can remember that when we applied for leave to use the deserted villas to put our sick soldiers into—the hospitals being full—we were told that it could only be done by private treaty with the owners, who were at that time on commando against us. I remember also suggesting that the corrugated-iron fencing round the cricket field should be used for making huts, and being told that it was impossible, as it was private property.

The same extreme respect for personal property was shown during Lord Roberts's advance. The country through which he passed swarmed with herds and flocks, but, with as scrupulous a regard for the rights of property as Wellington showed in the south of France, no hungry soldier was allowed to take so much as a chicken. The punishment for looting was prompt and stern. It is true that farms were burned occasionally and the stock confiscated, but this was as a punishment for some particular offence and not part of a system. The limping Tommy looked askance at the fat geese which covered the dam by the roadside, but it was as much as his life was worth to allow his fingers to close round those tempting white necks. On foul water and bully beef he tramped through a land of plenty.

A most striking example of British discipline and forbearance was furnished at this period, while the war could still be called regular upon the Boer side, by Rundle's Division, christened the 'Hungry Eighth' by the Army. This Division had the misfortune to be stationed for several months some distance from the railway line, and in consequence had great difficulty in getting supplies. They were on half-rations for a considerable period, and the men were so reduced in strength that their military efficiency was much impaired. Yet they lived in a land of plenty—a land of large farms well stocked with every sort of food. Why it was impossible to get this food for the men I do not know, but I do know that the prices for bread, eggs, milk, and other such things were kept very high by the wives of the farmers who were away upon commando; and that the hungry soldiers were quite unable to buy, and were not permitted to take, the nourishment which was essential.

On May 19, while Lord Roberts's force was advancing on Pretoria, De Wet sent in a despatch to complain of the destruction of two farms, Paarde Kraal and Leeuw Kop. Lord Roberts replied that these two farms were destroyed because, while a white flag was flying from the houses, the troops were fired upon from the farmsteads. 'I have had two farms near Kroonstad,' he adds, 'destroyed for similar reasons, and shall continue to punish all such cases of treachery by the destruction of the farms where they occur.' Here is a definite declaration of policy, quite distinct from wanton destruction, and it is difficult to see how any General could take any other steps, with justice to his own men. These farms, and all which are included in this category, were justly and properly destroyed—the families being removed without violence to a place of safety.

The next representations from the Boer Commander were more definite in their nature.

'Complaints are repeatedly reaching me,' he writes, 'that private dwellings are plundered, and in some cases totally destroyed, and all provisions taken from women and children, so that they are compelled to wander about without food or covering. To quote several instances: It has just been brought to my notice by way of sworn affidavit that the house of Field-Cornet S. Buys on the farm, Leeuwspruit district, Middelburg, was set on fire and destroyed on 20th June last. His wife, who was at home, was given five minutes' time to remove her bedding and clothing, and even what she took out was again taken from her. Her food, sugar, &c., was all taken, so that for herself and her children she had neither covering nor food for the following night. She was asked for the key of the safe, and after it was given up by her she was threatened with a sword, and money was demanded. All the money that was in the house was taken away, all the papers in the safe were torn up, and everything at the homestead that could not be taken away was destroyed. The house of Field-Cornet Buys's son was also destroyed, the doors and windows broken, &c.

'It has also been reported to me that my own buildings, on the farm Varkenspruit, district Standerton, as well as the house of Field-Cornet Badenhorst, on the adjoining farm, have been totally destroyed, and such of the stock as was not removed was shot dead on the farm.

'Further, there is the sworn declaration of Mrs. Hendrik Badenhorst, which speaks for itself.

'I cannot believe that such godless barbarities take place with Your Excellency's consent, and thus I deem it my solemn duty to protest most strongly against such destruction and vindictiveness as being entirely contrary to civilised warfare.'

The greater part of these alleged outrages had occurred on General Buller's side of the Transvaal, so the matter was referred to him. He acknowledged that he had ordered six farmhouses to be destroyed:

'The following circumstances induced me to give the order. On entering the Transvaal I caused the attached Proclamation (A) to be widely distributed along my line of route. We marched from Volksrust to Standerton practically unopposed. Shortly after our arrival at Standerton our telegraph line was cut on several nights following, and attempts were made to damage the military line by placing dynamite cartridges with detonators attached upon it. These attempts were all made on or in close vicinity to the estates above named. A watch was kept and it was found that the attempts were made not by any formed force of the enemy, but by a few scattered banditti who were given shelter during the night in the houses I afterwards had destroyed, and who thence, when they could, tried to murder our patrols, and sallied out at night to damage the line. It was further ascertained that these men came and usually returned through Varkenspruit. I directed that copies of Proclamation (A) should be personally left at each house, and the inmates of each should be warned that these depredations could not be permitted, and that if people living under our protection allowed these sort of men to resort to their houses without informing us, they must take the consequences, and their houses would be destroyed. This warning had some effect for a day or two, but on 1st and 2nd of July the nuisance recommenced, and on the 7th July, having acquired full proof that the houses were being regularly used as shelters for men who were hostile to us, and who were not under any proper command, in fact, who were only acting as banditti, I had the houses destroyed.

'The women and children occupying the farms were removed elsewhere with as little inconvenience to themselves as we could arrange.'

Here again it is impossible to doubt that the British commanders were well within their rights. It is true that Article XXIII of The Hague Conventions makes it illegal to destroy the enemy's property, but it adds: 'Unless such destruction be imperatively demanded by the necessities of war.' Now nothing can be more imperative in war than the preservation of the communications of the army. A previous clause of the same Article makes it illegal to 'kill or wound treacherously individuals belonging to the hostile army.' It is incontestable that to take the cover of a farmhouse which flies the white flag in order to make attacks is to 'kill or wound treacherously,' and so on a double count the action of the British becomes legal, and even inevitable. Lord Roberts's message to De Wet upon August 3, 1900, restates both his intentions and his reasons for it:

'Latterly, many of my soldiers have been shot from farmhouses over which the white flag has been flying, the railway and telegraph lines have been cut, and trains wrecked. I have therefore found it necessary, after warning your Honour, to take such steps as are sanctioned by the customs of war to put an end to these and similar acts, and have burned down the farmhouses at or near which such deeds have been perpetrated. This I shall continue to do whenever I consider the occasion demands it.

'The remedy lies in your Honour's own hands. The destruction of property is most distasteful to me, and I shall be greatly pleased when your Honour's co-operation in the matter renders it no longer necessary.'

This raises the question of the legality of the burning of farmhouses in the vicinity of the place where the railway is cut. The question presented itself forcibly to my mind when I saw with my own eyes the tall plumes of smoke rising from six farmhouses, De Wet's among them, in the neighbourhood of Roodeval. There is no doubt whatever that in the war of 1870—the classic type of modern war—the villages and populations near the scene of a cut railway were severely punished. But The Hague Conventions had not then been signed. On the one hand, it may be urged that it is impossible without such disciplinary measures to preserve a line of 1,000 miles running all the way through a hostile or semi-hostile country. Also that it is 'imperatively demanded by the necessities of war.' On the other hand, there is Article L., which says, 'No general penalty can be inflicted on the population on account of the acts of individuals, for which it cannot be regarded as collectively responsible.' An argument might be advanced for either side, but what will actually determine is the strongest argument of all—that of self-preservation. An army situated as the British Army was, and dependent for its supplies upon its communications, *must* keep them open even if it strains the Conventions in doing so. As a matter of fact, farm-burning had no effect in checking the railway-cutting, and had a considerable effect in embittering the population. Yet a General who was cut off from his base thirty times in a month was bound to leave the argument of legality to the jurists, and to adopt the means which seemed most likely to stop the nuisance. The punishment fell with cruel injustice upon some individuals. Others may have been among the actual raiders.

On September 2 Lord Roberts communicated his intentions to General Botha:

'SIR,—I have the honour to address your Honour regarding the operations of those comparatively small bands of armed Boers who conceal themselves on farms in the neighbourhood of our lines of communication and thence endeavour to damage the railway, thus endangering the lives of passengers travelling by train who may or may not be combatants.

'2. My reason for again referring to this subject is that, except in the districts occupied by the Army under the personal command of your Honour, there is now no formed body of Boer troops in the Transvaal or Orange River Colony, and that the war is degenerating into operations carried on by irregular and irresponsible guerillas. This would be so ruinous to the country and so deplorable from every point of view, that I feel bound to do everything in my power to prevent it.

'3. The orders I have at present issued, to give effect to these views, are that the farm nearest the scene of any attempt to injure the line or wreck a train is to be burnt, and that all farms within a radius of 10 miles are to be completely cleared of all their stock, supplies, &c.'

Granting that the penalty is legal at all, it must be allowed that it is put in a minimum form, since only one farm in each case is to be destroyed; and the further clearing of stock is undoubtedly justified, since it would tend to cripple the mobility of Boer raiders approaching the line. Yet one farm for each attack becomes a formidable total when the attacks are on an average of one per day.

We have treated two causes for which farms were burned: (1) For being used as cover for snipers; (2) as a punishment for the cutting of railways. A third cause now comes to the front. A large number of burghers had taken the oath of neutrality and had been allowed to return to their farms by the British. These men were persuaded or terrorised by the fighting commandos into breaking their parole and abandoning those farms on which they had sworn to remain. The farmhouses were their bail, and Lord Roberts decreed that it was forfeited. On August 23 he announced his decision to General Botha:

'Your Honour represents that well-disposed families living on their farms have been driven from their houses, and that their property has been taken away or destroyed. This no doubt is true, but not in the sense which your letter would imply. Burghers who are well-disposed towards the British Government, and anxious to submit to my authority, have had their property seized by the Boer commandos, and have been threatened with death if they refused to take up arms against the British forces. Your Honour's contention that a solemn oath of neutrality which the burghers have voluntarily taken in order to remain in unmolested occupation of their farms is null and void, because you have not consented to it, is hardly open to discussion. I shall punish those who violate their oath and confiscate their property, no burgher having been forced to take the oath against his will.'

It is quite certain that the Boer Government committed a very clear breach of the Conventions of The Hague in compelling, or even in permitting, these men to rejoin the ranks. 'In such cases,' says Article X., 'their own Government shall not require of, nor accept from, them any service incompatible with the parole given.' This is clear as regards the Government. But in the case of the men it is different. Their promise was in a sense conditional upon effective protection from our troops. We had no right to place a man in so terrible a position that he had to choose between breaking his parole and death at the hands of his own countrymen. If we were not sure that we could protect them, we could have retained them in guarded camps, as we eventually did. If we chose to turn them loose upon the wide veldt, then it was our fault more than theirs that they were forced into the ranks of the enemy. To their credit be it said that even under such pressure many of them were true to their oath.

But if their guilt is indeed no greater than our own, then how are we justified in burning down their houses? It seems to me that these cases are very different from those in the other two categories, and that the question of compensation to these men should be at least considered. I take it that the numerous cases where 'on commando' is marked against a burned farm on the official list, means that he had returned to commando after giving his parole. The destruction of his house under those circumstances is, in the peculiar conditions of the case, a harsh measure, but if 'on commando' means simply that the man was away doing his duty to his country, without any question of parole, then our conscience can never permit that man to go without compensation.

We can trace in this account of the communications between the leaders the growth of those harsher measures which have been so generally deplored in this country. So long as the war was regular it is certain that nothing could be more regular than the British conduct. When, however, the war became irregular upon the part of the Boers, and their army dissolved into small bands which harried the lines of communications, the small posts, and the convoys, there was a corresponding change upon the part of the troops. Towards the end of the year 1900 that change was pushed to considerable lengths. Certain districts which had been Boer centres, where they habitually collected time after time, were devastated and destroyed. Such districts were those of Kroonstad, Heilbron, Ventersburg, and Winburg. In these four districts about one hundred and seventy houses were destroyed. The village of Bothaville, which was a depôt of the enemy, was also destroyed. It consisted of forty-three houses. In the Transvaal the number of houses actually destroyed for strategic purposes seems to have been very much smaller. In the official returns only about twelve houses are so mentioned. Altogether the houses which have been burned for reasons which are open to dispute, including those of the men upon commando, do not appear to exceed two hundred and fifty.

It must be confessed that the case of these houses is entirely different from the others which have been destroyed, because they were used for active warlike operations. Of the 630 buildings which we know to have been destroyed, more than half have been used by snipers, or in some other direct fashion have brought themselves within the laws of warfare.

But it cannot be said that these others have done so. The cost of the average farmhouse is a mere trifle. A hundred pounds would build a small one, and 300£ a large. If we take the intermediate figure, then the expenditure of 50,000£. would compensate for those cases where military policy and international law may have been at variance with each other. The burning of houses ceased in the year 1900, and, save in very special instances, where there was an overwhelming military necessity, it has not been resorted to since. In the sweeping of the country carried out by French in the Eastern Transvaal and by Blood to the north of the Delagoa Railway, no buildings appear to have been destroyed, although it was a military necessity to clear the farms of every sort of supply in order to hamper the movements of the commandos. The destruction of the crops and herds of the Boers, distasteful as such work must be, is exactly analogous to the destruction by them of our supply trains on which the Army depended for their food. Guerilla warfare cannot enjoy all its own advantages and feel none of its own defects. It is a two-edged weapon, and the responsibility for the consequences rests upon the combatant who first employs it.

VII. THE CONCENTRATION CAMPS

When considerable districts of the country were cleared of food in order to hamper the movements of the commandos, and when large numbers of farmhouses were destroyed under the circumstances already mentioned, it became evident that it was the duty of the British, as a civilised people, to form camps of refuge for the women and children, where, out of reach, as we hoped, of all harm, they could await the return of peace. There were three courses open. The first was to send the Boer women and children into the Boer lines—a course which became impossible when the Boer army broke into scattered bands and had no longer any definite lines; the second was to leave them where they were; the third was to gather them together and care for them as best we could.

It is curious to observe that the very people who are most critical of the line of policy actually adopted, were also most severe when it appeared that the alternative might be chosen. The British nation would have indeed remained under an ineffaceable stain had they left women and children without shelter upon the veldt in the presence of a large Kaffir population. Even Mr. Stead could hardly have ruined such a case by exaggeration. On some rumour that it would be so, he drew harrowing pictures of the moral and physical degradation of the Boer women in the vicinity of the British camps. No words can be too strong to stigmatise such assertions unless the proof of them is overwhelmingly strong—and yet the only 'proof' adduced is the bare assertion of a partisan writer in a partisan paper, who does not claim to have any personal knowledge of the matter. It is impossible without indignation to know that a Briton has written on such evidence of his own fellow-countrymen that they have 'used famine as a pander to lust.'

Such language, absurd as it is, shows very clearly the attacks to which the British Government would have been subjected had they *not* formed the camps of refuge. It was not merely that burned-out families must be given a shelter, but it was that no woman on a lonely farm was safe amid a black population, even if she had the means of procuring food. Then, again, we had learned our lesson as regards the men who had given their parole. They should not again be offered the alternative of breaking their oaths or being punished by their own people. The case for the formation of the camps must be admitted to be complete and overwhelming. They were formed, therefore, by the Government at convenient centres, chiefly at Pretoria, Johannesburg, Krugersdorp, Middelburg, Potchefstroom, Rustenburg, Heidelburg, Standerton, Pietersburg, Klerksdorp, and Volksrust in the Transvaal; Bloemfontein, Kroonstad, Bethulie, and Edenburg in the Orange Free State.

Such camps as refuges were no new things, for the British refugees from Johannesburg have been living for over a year in precisely such places. As no political capital and no international sentiment could be extracted from their sufferings, and as they have borne their troubles with dignity and restraint, we have heard little of the condition of their lives, which is in many ways more deplorable than that of the Boers.

Having determined to form the camps, the authorities carried out the plan with great thoroughness. The sites seem to have been well chosen, and the arrangements in most cases all that could be wished. They were formed, however, at an unfortunate moment. Great strain had been placed upon our Commissariat by the large army, over 200,000 men, who had to be supplied by three tiny railways, which were continually cut. In January 1901 De Wet made his invasion of Cape Colony, and the demand upon the lines was excessive. The extraordinary spectacle was presented at that time of the British straining every nerve to feed the women and children of the enemy, while that enemy was sniping the engineers and derailing the trains which were bringing up the food.

The numbers of the inmates of the refugee camps increased rapidly from 20,000 at the end of the year 1900, up to more than 100,000 at the end of 1901. Great efforts were made by the military authorities to accommodate the swelling tide of refugees, and no money was spared for that purpose. Early in the year 1901 a painful impression was created in England by the report of Miss Hobhouse, an English lady, who had visited the camps and criticised them unfavourably. The value of her report was discounted, however, by the fact that her political prejudices were known to be against the Government. Mr. Charles Hobhouse, a relation of hers, and a Radical member of Parliament, has since then admitted that some of her statements will not bear examination. With the best will in the world her conclusions would have been untrustworthy, since she could speak no Dutch, had no experience of the Boer character, and knew nothing of the normal conditions of South African life.

Her main contentions were that the diet was not sufficient, that there was little bedding, that the water-supply was short, that the sanitation was bad, that there was overcrowding, and that there was an excessive death-rate, especially among the children.

As to diet, the list which she gives agrees roughly with that which is officially quoted as the daily allowance at Irene Camp, near Pretoria, in July. It is as follows:

Meat 1/2 lb. Coffee 2 oz. Flour 3/4 lb. Sugar 2 oz. Salt 1/2 oz. To every child under six, a bottle of milk

It must be confessed that the diet is a spare one, and that as supplies become more plentiful it might well be increased. The allowance may, however, be supplemented by purchase, and there is a considerable outside fund, largely subscribed by British people, which is used to make the scale more liberal. A slight difference was made at first between the diet of a family which had surrendered and of that the head of which was still in arms against us. A logical distinction may certainly be made, but in practice it was felt to be unchivalrous and harsh, so it was speedily abandoned.

As to the shortness of the water-supply, it is the curse of all South Africa, which alternately suffers from having too much water and too little. With artesian wells and better arrangements this difficulty is being overcome, but it has applied as strongly to our own camps as to those of the Boer refugees.

There seems to be a consensus of opinion from all the camps that the defects in sanitation are due to the habits of the inmates, against which commandants and doctors are perpetually fighting. Camp life without cleanliness must become unhygienic. The medical reports are filled with instances of the extreme difficulty which has been experienced in enforcing discipline upon those who have been accustomed to the absolute liberty of the lonely veldt.

On the question of overcrowding, the demand for tents in South Africa has been excessive, and it may well have taxed all the power of the authorities to find accommodation for the crowds of women and children. The evil has been remedied since the time of Miss Hobhouse's report. It is well known that the Boers in their normal life have no objection to crowded rooms, and that the inmates of a farmhouse are accustomed to conditions which would be unendurable to most. To overcrowd a tent is hygienically almost impossible, for the atmosphere of a tent, however crowded, will never become tainted in the same sense as a room.

All these things are of human contrivance, and the authorities were doing their best to set them right, as Miss Hobhouse herself acknowledged. 'They are, I believe, doing their best with very limited means,' said she, and in so saying reduced her whole report to nothing. For if they are really doing their best, then what more can be said? The only alternative is the breaking up of the camps and the dispersal of the women. But in that case Mr. Stead is waiting for us with some 'Blood and Hell' broadsheet to tell us of the terrible fate of those women upon the veldt. It must be one or the other. Of the two I prefer Miss Hobhouse and the definite grievances which she reports, to the infinite possibilities of Mr. Stead. As to the suggestion that this enormous crowd of women and children should be quartered upon their kinsmen in the Colony, it is beyond all argument. There has been no offer of such wholesale hospitality nor have we any means for enforcing it.

But then we come to the great and piteous tragedy of the refugee camps, the mortality, and especially the mortality among the children. That is deplorable—more deplorable even than the infant mortality in Mafeking, Ladysmith, and Kimberley. But is it avoidable? Or is it one of those misfortunes, like that enteric outbreak which swept away so many British soldiers, which is beyond our present sanitary science and can only be endured with sad resignation? The nature of the disease which is mainly responsible for the high mortality shows that it has no direct connection with the sanitary conditions of the camps, or with anything which it was in our power to alter. Had the deaths come from some filth-disease, such as typhus fever, or even from enteric or diphtheria, the sanitation of the camps might be held responsible. But it is to a severe form of measles that the high mortality is due. Apart from that the record of the camps would have been a very fair one. Now measles when once introduced among children runs through a community without any regard to diet or conditions of life. The only possible hope is the segregation of the sufferer. To obtain this early quarantine the co-operation of the parent is needed: but in the case in point the Boer mothers, with a natural instinct, preferred to cling to the children and to make it difficult for the medical men to remove them in the first stages of the disease. The result was a rapid spread of the epidemic, which was the more fatal as many of the sufferers were in low health owing to the privations unavoidably endured in the journey from their own homes to the camps. Not only was the spread of the disease assisted by the mother, but in her mistaken zeal she frequently used remedies which were as fatal as the disease. Children died of arsenical-poisoning, having been covered from head to foot with green paint; and others of opium-poisoning, having quack drugs which contain laudanum administered to them. 'In Potchefstroom as at Irene,' says Dr. Kendal Franks, 'the death-rate is attributable not so much to the severity of the epidemic as to the ignorance, perverseness, and dirty habits of the parents themselves.' But whatever the immediate cause the death of these numerous children lies heavy, not upon the conscience, but upon the heart of our nation. It is some mitigation to know that the death-rate among children is normally quite remarkably high in South Africa, and that the rate in the camps was frequently not higher than that of the towns near which the camp was situated.

Be this as it may, we cannot deny that the cause of the outbreak of measles was the collection of the women and children by us into the camps. But why were they collected into camps? Because they could not be left on the veldt. And why could they not be left on the veldt? Because we had destroyed the means of subsistence. And why had we destroyed the means of subsistence? To limit the operations of the mobile bands of guerillas. At the end of every tragedy we are forced back to the common origin of all of them, and made to understand that the nation which obstinately perseveres in a useless guerilla war prepares much trouble for its enemy, but absolute ruin for itself.

We have pushed our humanity in this matter of the refugees so far that we have looked after our enemies far better than our friends. I recognise that the two cases are not on all fours, since the Boers are compelled to be in camps and the loyalist refugees are not. But the fact remains that the loyalists *are* in camps, through no fault of their own, and that their condition is a worse one than that of our enemies. At East London, for example, there are two refugee camps, Boer and British. The former has 350, the latter 420 inhabitants. The former are by far the better fed, clad, and housed, with a hospital, a school, and a washhouse, all of which are wanting in the British camp. At Port Elizabeth there is a Boer camp. A Dutch deputation came with 50£ to expend in improving their condition, but returned without spending the money as nothing was needed. The Boer refugees and the British are catered for by the same man at Port Elizabeth. He is allowed 15*d* per head for the Boers per day, and 8*d* for the British. These are the 'Methods of Barbarism.'

I shall now take a few opinions of the camps from British sources and from Boer. I have only seen one British witness who was in sympathy with Miss Hobhouse, and that is a lady (name not mentioned) who is quoted in the appendix of Mr. Methuen's 'Peace or War.' She takes much the same view, insisting mainly upon the insufficient diet, the want of fuel and of bed-clothing. Against these two ladies I shall very shortly and in condensed form cite a few witnesses from both sides.

Mr. Seaton, of Johannesburg (Secretary of the Congregational Church and of the burgher camp), says: 'The reports you send make our blood boil. They are frightfully exaggerated, and in many instances not only misleading but untrue.... A more healthy spot it would be difficult to find.... There is no overcrowding.

'Some weeks ago there was an epidemic of measles in camp of a very severe type, and naturally there were many deaths among the children. The doctor and nurses worked to the very utmost, and I am pleased to say the epidemic is stamped out. No doubt this is what caused the talk by the pro-Boers in the House of Commons and elsewhere, but it is one of those epidemics which could not be prevented among the class of people we have here. They had absolutely no regard for sanitary conveniences, and the officials had the greatest difficulty in enforcing the most ordinary rules of cleanliness. Another difficulty we had was to get them to bring their children when sick into the hospital, where there is every convenience. They prefer to disobey the doctor and try the old women's remedies, which, as you know, are very plentiful among such people. The doctor has had a most trying position, and has worked like a slave. Nearly all the deaths have been from measles. We are having a fairly mild winter. About three months ago it was bitterly cold, but they are used to outdoor life, and this is no worse than they have always been used to. The tents are all military tents, and there is no sign of leakage. I know they all want tents when they come here, if it is possible to get them. On the whole, the inmates are contented, and the children are particularly happy. They skip and play about from morn till eve.'

The Rev. R. Rogers (Wesleyan minister) writes:

'What is the use of persons ignorant of the life and customs of the Boers coming to investigate these burgher camps? I have seen, and do not hesitate to say, that most of them are better housed, better clothed, and better fed than in their own homes of wattle and daub, and mud floors.'

Mr. Howe of the Camp Soldiers' Homes says:

'We do not pass judgment; we only state facts.

'When the first concentration camp was formed we were on the spot, and also saw others spring up. We admit that there has been suffering, but we solemnly affirm that the officers in charge of the several camps known to us were only too anxious to make the helpless people as comfortable as possible. We have seen the huge cases and bales of comforts for the inmates, and know that, in order to expedite the despatch of these things, military stores and ordnance have been kept back.'

The Rev. R. B. Douglas (Presbyterian minister) writes:

'I am glad to see that you are not giving credence to the tales of brutality and cruelty which are being freely circulated by disloyal agitators about the treatment of the Boer refugees. But one point on which you ask for more information is worth being noticed—the difference of treatment between families of those on commando and others. I am in a position to state that the whole difference made amounted to two ounces of coffee and four ounces of sugar per week, and that even this distinction totally disappeared by the middle of March. As a set-off to this, the local Dutch Committee, in distributing some sixty cases of clothing, &c., sent out by the charitable, refused to give any help to the families of some who were not on commando, on the ground that these articles were for the benefit of those who were fighting for their country.'

Mrs. Gauntlett, of Johannesburg, writes:

'I have read certain statements you sent me from English papers on cruelty to Boer refugee families. I am amazed at the iniquity of men who circulate such lies, and the credulity of those who believe them. The opinion of Germans, French, Americans, and even many Dutch, here on the spot, is that the leniency and amazing liberality of the Government to their foes is prolonging the war. A Dutch girl in the Pretoria Camp declared to the nurse that for seven months they had not been able to get such good food as was given them by the British.'

Mr. Soutar, Secretary of the Pretoria Camp, writes:

'The Boer women and children get as much food as they require, and have all sorts of medical comforts, such as beef-tea, extracts of meat, jellies, brandy and wine, and the advantage of fully qualified attendants. Not only are their absolute requirements provided for, but even their "fads" are considered.'

Mr. Scholtz, Inspector of Camps for the Transvaal, reports:

'Many of the children, when they first arrived at the camp, were little better than skin and bone, and, being in so emaciated a condition, it was not surprising that, when they did catch measles, they could not cope with the disease. Many of the women would not open their tents to admit fresh air, and, instead of giving the children the proper medicines supplied by the military, preferred to give them home remedies. The mothers would not sponge the children, and the greatest difficulty was experienced in inducing them to send the patients to hospital. The cause of the high death-rate among children from measles is due to the fact that the women let their children out as soon as the measles rash has subsided. Pneumonia and bronchitis naturally supervene. Another cause is that the mothers persist in giving their children meat and other indigestible foods, even when the doctors strictly prohibit it, dysentery resulting as a matter of course. In other respects the health of the camp is good, there being only one case of typhoid out of 5,000 residents in camp.'

Here is light on the Krugersdorp Camp:

'JOHAO8ESBURG, July 31st.—(Reuter's Special Service.)—Commandant Alberts, commanding the Boers near Krugersdorp, has sent a letter to the officer commanding the British forces at Krugersdorp, stating that as he has with him on commando several families whose male relatives have recently surrendered, he wishes to know if he will receive these families, as they would like to go to Krugersdorp. The officer replied that he would be pleased to receive them, and they are expected to arrive to-day.

'This action on the part of the Boers clearly shows that the families themselves have no longer any objection to the Refugee Camps, where everything is done to promote their comfort, or any disinclination to being placed under our care and protection.'

From Reuter's agent at Springfontein:

'I to-day visited the Boer Refugee Camp here, containing 2,700 inmates. The camp is splendidly situated, and well laid out. I spoke to several refugees, and met with no complaint, all being satisfied with the treatment received. The hospital arrangements are excellent, and there is very little sickness in the camp.'

From Mr. Celliers, Dutch Minister from Aberdeen, Cape Colony, sent to inspect the Port Elizabeth Refugee Camp:

'He was writing this to show that the British Government were doing everything in their power to help the exiles, and to show that, although these exiles' relatives and friends were still in the field, yet the powers were merciful and kind to the exiles, showing them no enmity, for which they felt grateful. He wished the people to understand that he was at liberty to speak to them privately, and that he had a fair opportunity to hear any complaints, if there were any to be made. Mr. Hess allowed him to go round, placing full confidence in him, and he felt satisfied that if there had been anything wrong he should have heard of it. It had been his opinion all along that the Military, in sending these exiles down there, had done so for their own safety and advantage; and that it had preserved them, and been a blessing in disguise, which would be acknowledged by all in time to come.'

Major Harold Sykes's (2nd Dragoons) evidence is reported as follows:

He arranged the first of the Refugee Concentrated Camps, and when he left he had a camp of about six thousand women and children under his care. All charges of cruelty and inhumanity were vile and calumnious falsehoods. Nay, worse, they were miserable, despicable concoctions. Both women and children were better off, the great bulk of them, than ever they were in their lives. The only thing approaching cruelty to them was at the authorities insisted upon cleanliness and proper attention to sanitary regulations, which the average Boer, being a stranger to, utterly disliked. He had seen all the workings of these camps. He could give an unqualified denial to all the villainous allegations that had recently been made in public meeting and in the House of Commons.

Under date November 1, an officer of the Kroonstad Camp writes:

'We have cricket, tennis, and croquet for them, and they are all jolly well treated. Besides other amusements, they have a band twice a week, and the other day they got up a concert.'

This is what Mr. Stead calls 'doing to death by slow torture all the women and children whom we have penned behind the barbed wire of our prison camps.' Can a cause be a sound one which is pleaded in such terms!

Now for some Boer voices.

Commandant Alberts writes:

'Major WALTER, Boksburg.—Honoured Sir,—I must express to you and the other officers of Boksburg my heartfelt thanks for the great kindness shown towards my wife, and at the same time for the message, and I hope that this kindness may sometime be repaid to you.

'May you and I be spared to have a personal meeting.

'I have the honour to be your honour's servant,

'(Signed) H. ALBERTS, Commandant.'

A Dutch minister writes to Captain SNOWDEN, O.C. of Boer Camp, Johannesburg:—'Sir,—I am directed by the Committee of the Dutch Reformed Churches here to convey to you the appreciation of the Committee for the kindly interest and sympathy shown by you to the women and children under your charge.'

One hundred male refugee Boers in the camp at Kroonstad sign the following sentiment:

'We also wish to tender Your Excellency our heartiest thanks for the interest you take in the education of our youth, and we trust you will succeed in your endeavours, and that the growing-up generation will be taught to be God-fearing, honest, and loyal citizens under the British flag. We regret, however, to state that, notwithstanding the highly appreciated efforts of our worthy superintendent and doctors, still so many cases of sickness and deaths occur daily in this camp, still we hope and trust Your Excellency will do all in your power for the health in this camp.

'We trust that the efforts of our worthy superintendent towards promoting our welfare under trying circumstances will be appreciated by Your Excellency. We are happy to state that the spirit of loyalty is daily increasing in this camp, and that the majority of the male refugees have taken the oath of allegiance.'

Mr. Dudley Keys, a surrendered burgher, writes to his brother:

'I have been in camp now for more than seven months—a sufficient time, you will allow, for reflection—and the immutability of the life provides ample scope for indulgence in that direction. How we long for the settlement you cannot imagine, nor can you imagine with what disgust and impatience we regard every endeavour on the part of the pro-Boers, as they are called, to divert the natural and inevitable course of things. You will not be surprised at hearing this from a one-time Dutch Republican when you take into consideration that all of us who have surrendered are fully aware of the fact that we were the aggressors, and that our statesmen are to blame for our present predicament. A large number of Boers, of course, will never come to view the matter in this light. That, of course, is not the result of thought and reflection, but utter and total ignorance. When Miss Hobhouse was here I frequently saw her priming herself or being primed. Some of our women would tell her anything for a dress or a pair of boots. If she knew our countrymen and women as well as we know them, her story would have been a short one. Now the home Government are despatching this commission. Well, when they see the women and children in camp they will naturally feel sorry for them. Who would not? But if they only remember that this is war and not a picnic, they will satisfy the people in England on their return that all we want is peace, and plenty of it.'

He adds:

'In spite of the lack of gratitude shown by our people, the authorities continue to make improvements and to lessen the hardships. That this entails enormous expenditure you will see by the statistics frequently published in the English papers. When I hear our people grumble, I often wonder how they would have treated the Britishers if the positions were reversed, and I am bound to acknowledge that it would not compare favourably with the treatment we receive.'

A Boer woman, writing from Pietermaritzburg, says:

'Those who complain of anything must lie, for we are in good circumstances.'

In a second letter she says:

'I can make no complaint at all.'

Mrs. Blignant, writing from the Port Elizabeth Refugee Camp, says:

'If we had to complain it would be false complaint, and all the stories about ill-treatment are untrue as far as I can find out.' Among the women cared for in this camp was one from Jagersfontein, who boasted—and with truth—that she had shot two unarmed British soldiers with a revolver.

Such is some of the evidence to be placed against Miss Hobhouse's report, and that of the unnamed lady in Pretoria. In justice it must be acknowledged that some camps may have been more open to criticism than others, and that (as we should expect) they became more perfect with time. But I cannot believe that any impartial mind can read the evidence without seeing that the British Government was doing its best under difficult circumstances to carry out the most humane plan possible, and that any other must involve consequences from which a civilised nation must shrink.

Towards the end of 1901 an attempt was made to lessen the mortality in the camps by bringing them down to the sea-coast. The problem was complicated by the fact that many of the refugees were averse from leaving their own country, and had come in upon a promise that they would not be asked to do so. Those who would were moved down, and the camps at East London, Port Elizabeth, and Merebank, near Durban, largely increased. 'No expense must be allowed to stand in the way,' said Mr. Chamberlain in an official message. In Blue Book (Cd. 853) we find Lord Milner and the Colonial Secretary discussing every means by which the mortality might be lessened and the comfort of the camps increased.

It is worthy of record that the portrait of an emaciated child has been circulated upon the Continent and in America as a proof positive of the horrors of the concentration system. It is only too probable that there are many emaciated children in the camps, for they usually arrive in that condition. This particular portrait however was, as I am credibly informed, taken by the British authorities on the occasion of the criminal trial of the mother for the ill-usage of the child. The incident is characteristic of the unscrupulous tactics which have been used from the beginning to poison the mind of the world against Great Britain.

VIII. THE BRITISH SOLDIER IN SOUTH AFRICA

When Lord Roberts desired to sum up the character of the soldiers whom he had led, he declared that they had behaved like gentlemen. I believe that statement to be no exaggeration, and I think that when the bitter animosities of warfare have subsided, it will be acknowledged by the Boers themselves that it is true. They have had some unsavoury work to do—for guerilla warfare brings much in its train which is hateful—but officers and men have ameliorated and softened the asperities of warfare wherever it has been possible to do so. Their character has been most foully attacked by politicians at home, and by the ignorant or malevolent abroad. Let us examine the evidence.

There were many military attachés present with our Army. Have any of them reported against the discipline of our soldiers? So far as their reports are known, nothing of the sort has been alleged. Captain Slocum, the American representative, writes from Bloemfontein:

'The British have been too merciful, and I believe, had a more rigorous course been adopted when the Army first entered this capital and the enemy thoroughly stampeded, the war would have been materially shortened.'

The French military attaché said: 'What I admire most in this campaign is the conduct of your soldiers. Here they are trekking and fighting daily in an uninteresting country, scorched by day, cold by night, without drink, without women. Any other soldiers in Europe would have mutinied long ago.'

There were several foreign war-correspondents with our army. Of these the only Frenchman, M. Carrère of the 'Matin' was an ardent pro-Boer. Read his book, 'En pleine Epopée.' He is bitter against our policy and our politicians. His eyes are very keenly open for flaws in our Army. But from cover to cover he has nothing but praise for the devoted Tommy and his chivalrous officer.

Three American correspondents were there—there may have been more, but three I knew. These were Messrs. Julian Ralph, James Barnes, and Unger. The first two were much impressed by the humanity and discipline of the British troops, though Mr. Ralph was, I believe, like Captain Slocum, of the opinion that it was occasionally pushed too far. Mr. Unger's published impressions of the war confirm the same idea.

Here, then, is practical unanimity among all the impartial witnesses. On the opinions of our own correspondents I will not dwell. I have the advantage of knowing nearly all of them, and though among them are several gentlemen who have a chivalrous and idealistic sympathy for the Boers, I cannot recollect that I have ever once heard one of them record a single instance where they had been shocked by the conduct of a soldier.

I may, perhaps, be permitted to add my own testimony. I went to South Africa with great sympathy for the individual Boer, and with a belief that I should find soldiers in the field very different from soldiers in peace. I was three months in Bloemfontein when there were from ten to thirty thousand men encamped round the town. During that time I only once saw a man drunk. I never saw a man drunk during the short time that I was in Pretoria and Johannesburg. I once heard of a soldier striking a Boer. It was because the man had refused to raise his hat at the burial of the soldier's comrade. I not only never saw any outrage, but in many confidential talks with officers I never heard of one. I saw twenty Boer prisoners within five minutes of their capture. The soldiers were giving them cigarettes. Only two assaults on women came to my ears while I was in Africa. In each case the culprit was a Kaffir, and the deed was promptly avenged by the British Army.

Miss Hobhouse has mixed with a great number of refugees, many of whom are naturally very bitter against us. She is not reticent as to the tales which they told her. Not one of them all has a story of outrage. One woman, she says, was kicked by a drunken soldier, for which, she adds, he was punished.

An inmate of the Springfontein Refugee Camp, Mr. Maltman, of Philippolis, writes: 'All the Boer women here speak in the highest terms of the treatment they have received at the hands of soldiers.'

Here is the testimony of a burgher's wife, Mrs. Van Niekirk:

'Will you kindly allow me to give my testimony to the kindly treatment of the Dutch women and children by the British troops? As the wife of a Transvaal burgher, I have lived in Krugersdorp since 1897, until three weeks ago. The town was taken in June last, and since then there has always been a fairly large force of men in, or quite near it; indeed, on several occasions the numbers have amounted to ten thousand, or more, and have been of many different regiments, English, Scotch, Irish, and Colonial.

'At such times the streets and the few shops open were thronged with soldiers, while, even when the town was quietest, there were always numbers of them about. The women were at first afraid, but they very soon discovered that they could move about as freely as in ordinary times, without fear of any annoyance. During the whole six months I never saw or heard of a single instance where a woman was treated with the slightest disrespect; the bearing of both officers and men was invariably deferential to all women, and kindly to children.

'Last July a detachment of Gordon Highlanders was camped on the veldt for a week in front of my house, which stands almost alone on the outskirts of the town. My husband was away during the time, and I was alone with my young children. The nearest camp-fires were not a dozen yards from my gate, yet I never experienced the least annoyance, nor missed from my ground even so much as a stick of wood.

'I could multiply instances, but after this little need be said; if I had not seen it I could not have believed that a victorious army would behave with such humanity and consideration in the territory of a people even then in arms against them; and if they behave so in Krugersdorp—a place mind you, where during the last six months their doings could not be openly criticised—is it likely that their conduct in other places will be so entirely different?—I am, &c.'

This is the testimony of a woman. Here it is from a man's point of view—an old burgher who had very special opportunities for studying the conduct of British troops:

'Allow me to state here, once for all, that throughout the entire war all the English officers—and a great many of all ranks came to see us—treated us with the greatest kindness and courtesy. They knew, too, that I was a burgher, and that I had several sons who were doing their duty in fighting for the independence of our country.

'I return once more to the conduct of "Tommy Atkins." We saw numbers of convoys, some of which were more than sixteen kilometres long, bringing a great many Boer prisoners and their families to Pretoria. Tommy was everywhere, watching the wagons, marching without a word in clouds of dust, frequently in mud to the ankle, never rough towards women or children, as has been so often repeated. We have heard the contrary stated by our tried friends and by our own children.

'During halts, Tommy was the best and readiest creature imaginable; he got the water boiled, laid himself out to attend to the children in a thousand ways, and comforted the broken-hearted mothers. His hand was ready with help for every invalid. At our farm he helped of his own free will in saving a drowning beast, or in removing a fat pig that had been killed, sometimes even in rounding-in cattle that had strayed out of bounds, and so on, giving help in a thousand ways. For all that he wanted no reward. Rewards he refused altogether simply because it was good-feeling which made him do these things.

'Sir, these are indisputable facts, which I have repeated as accurately as I could, leaving your readers to draw their own conclusions.

'OLD BURGHER OF THE TRANSVAAL.

'Rustenburg, Transvaal: July 1901.'

A long and curious letter appears in the 'Suisse Liberale' from a young Swiss who spent the whole time of the war upon a farm in the Thabanchu district of the Orange Free State. It is very impartial in its judgments, and remarks, among other things—talking of the life of the local garrison:

'They make frequent visits, send out invitations, and organise picnics. In the town they get up charity concerts, balls, sports, and horse-races. It is a curious thing that the English, even when they are at war, cannot live without their usual sports, and the conquered do not show the slightest repugnance to joining the victors in their games or to mixing in society with them.'

Is this consistent with stories of military brutality? It appears to be a very modified hell which is loose in that portion of Africa.

Mr. and Mrs. Osborn Howe were the directors of the Camp Soldiers' Homes in South Africa. They have seen as much of the army in South Africa as most people, and have looked at it with critical eyes. Here are some of their conclusions:

'Neither we nor our staff, scattered between De Aar and Pretoria, have ever heard of a single case of outrage or ill-treatment. One and all indignantly denied the accusations against our soldiers, and have given us many instances of great kindness shown by the troops towards helpless women and children.

'We ourselves saw nothing which we could not tell to a gathering of schoolgirls.

'When living in the Orange River Colony we were in the midst of the farm- burning district, and witnessed Lord Roberts's efforts to spare the people suffering by issuing warning proclamations. We saw how the officers waited till the farmers had had time to digest these repeated warnings, and then with what reluctance both officers and men went to carry out the work of destruction, but we never heard of a case where there had not first been some overt act on the part of the enemy.

'A story of reported outrage at a Dutch mission-house in the slums of a large town was found after personal investigation to have been anything but an outrage as the result proved. The young soldiers who entered the house when the door was opened in answer to their knock, withdrew after they had discovered that the ladies who occupied the house were missionaries, nor had anything been removed or injured. But the garbled story, with its misuse of the word "outrage," reached a district in Cape Colony where it did no little mischief in fanning the flames of animosity and rebellion. Thus the reported "outrage" was not even a common assault.

'It may be said that our love for the soldiers has warped our judgment. We would say we love God, and we love truth more than the honour of our soldiers. If there was another side we should not hide it.'

So much for the general facts. But it is notoriously difficult to prove a negative. Let us turn then to particular instances which have been raked together, and see what can be made of them. One of them occurred early in the war, when it was stated that there had been two assaults upon women in Northern Natal. Here are the lies duly nailed to the counter.

The Vicar of Dundee, Colony of Natal, on being requested by the Bishop of Natal to inquire into the truth of a statement that four women of a family near Dundee, named Bester, were outraged by English soldiers, reported that he had had an interview with the father-in-law of Bester, Jacobus Maritz, who is one of the most influential farmers in the district. Maritz said to him:

'Well, Mr. Bailey, you do right in coming to me, for our family (Mrs. Bester is his daughter) is the *only* family of Bester in the district, and you can say from me, that the story is nothing but a pack of lies.'

The other case, alleged at Dundee, furnished no names. The only thing specified was that one of the men was in the uniform of a Highlander. The Vicar replies to this: 'As you are aware, no Highland regiment has been stationed at Dundee during the war.'

The weapons of slander were blunted by the fact that about May 1900 the Transvaal Government, wishing to allay the fears of the women in the farms, published an announcement in the 'Volksstem' advising every burgher to leave his family upon the farms as the enemy were treating women and children with the utmost consideration and respect. We know that both President Kruger and General Botha acted up to this advice by leaving their own wives under our protection while they carried on their campaign against us. At the very instant that Kruger was falsely stating at Marseilles that we were making war on women and children, his own infirm wife was being so sedulously guarded by British soldiers that the passer-by was not even allowed to stare curiously at the windows or to photograph the house.

There was a lull in the campaign of calumny which was made up for by the whole-hearted effort of M. van Broekhuizen. This man was a minister in Pretoria, and, like most of the Dutch ministers, a red-hot politician. Having given his parole to restrain his sentiments, he was found to be still preaching inflammatory political sermons; so he was advised to leave, and given a passage gratis to Europe. He signalised his arrival by an article printed in the 'Independence Belge,' declaring among other statements that 30 per cent. of the Boer women had been ruined by the British troops. Such a statement from such a source raised a feeling of horror in Europe, and one of deep anger and incredulity on the side of those who knew the British Army. The letter was forwarded to Pretoria for investigation, and elicited the following unofficial comments from M. Constançon, the former Swiss Consul in that city, who had been present during the whole British occupation:

'I am more than astonished, I am disgusted, that a Lausanne paper should print such abominable and filthy lies.

'The whole article from the beginning to the end is nothing but a pack of lies, and the writer, a minister of the Gospel, of all men, ought to know better than to perjure himself and his office in the way he does.

'I have lived for the last eighteen years in or around Pretoria, and know almost every Boer family in the district. The two names mentioned by Broekhuizen of women assaulted by the troops are quite unknown to me, and are certainly not Boer names.

'Ever since the entry of the troops in the Transvaal, I have travelled constantly through the whole of Pretoria district and part of the Waterberg. I have often put up at Boer houses for the night, and stopped at all houses on my road on my business. In most of these houses the men were away fighting against the British; women and children alone were to be found on the farms. Nowhere and in no instance have I heard a single word of complaint against the troops; here and there a few fowls were missing and fencing poles pulled out for firewood; but this can only be expected from troops on the march. On the other hand, the women could not say enough in praise of the soldiers, and their behaviour towards their sex. Whenever a camp was established close to the homestead, the officers have always had a picket placed round the house for the object of preventing all pilfering, and the women, rich or poor, have everywhere been treated as ladies.

'Why the Boer women were so unanimous in their praises is because they were far from expecting such treatment at the hands of the victors.

'Our town is divided into wards, and every woman and child has been fed whenever they were without support, and in one ward we have actually five hundred of these receiving rations from the British Government, although in most cases the men are still fighting. In the towns the behaviour of the troops has been, admirable, all canteens have been closed, and in the last six months I have only seen two cases of drunkenness amongst soldiers.

'We are quite a little Swiss colony here, and I don't know one of my countrymen who would not endorse every word of my statement.

'Many may have sympathies with the Boers, but in all justice they will always give credit to the British troops and their officers for the humane way this war is carried on, and for the splendid way in which Tommy Atkins behaves himself.'

With this was printed in the 'Gazette de Lausanne,' which instituted the inquiry, a letter from Mr. Gray, Presbyterian minister in Pretoria, which says:

'A few days ago I received an extract from your issue of November 17 last entitled "La Civilisation Anglaise en Afrique." It consisted mainly of a letter over the signature of H. D. van Broekhuizen (not Broesehuizen as printed), Boer pastor of Pretoria. Allow me, sir, to assure you that the wholesale statements with regard to the atrocities of British soldiers contained in that letter are a tissue of falsehoods, and constitute an unfounded calumny which it would be difficult to parallel in the annals of warfare. It is difficult to conceive the motives that actuate the writer, but that they have been violent enough to make him absolutely reckless as to facts, is evident.

'When I got the article from your paper I immediately went out to make inquiry as to what possible foundation there was for the charges hurled so wildly at the British soldier. Having lived in Pretoria for the last eleven years I am acquainted with many of the local Boers. Those of them whom I questioned assured me that they had never known a case in which British soldiers had outraged a woman. One case was rumoured, but had never been substantiated, and was regarded as very doubtful. Let it be granted that some solitary cases of rudeness may have occurred, that would not be surprising under the circumstances. Still it would not furnish a ground for the libelling of a whole army. The astonishing fact is, however, that in this country one only hears of the surprise everywhere felt that the British soldier has been so self-restrained and deferential towards women.'

To this M. van Broekhuizen's feeble reply was that there was no ex-consul of the name of Constançon in Pretoria. The 'Gazette de Lausanne' then pointed out that the gentleman was well known, that he had acted in that capacity for many years, and added that if M. van Broekhuizen was so ill-informed upon so simple a matter, it was not likely that he was very correct upon other more contentious ones. Thus again a false coin was nailed to the counter, but only after it had circulated so widely that many who had passed it would never know that it was proved to be base metal. Incredible as it may seem, the infamous falsehood was repeated in 1902 by a Dr. Vallentin, in the 'Deutsche Rundschau,' from which it was copied into other leading German papers without any reference to its previous disproof in 1901.

Now we will turn for a moment to the evidence of Miss Alice Bron, the devoted Belgian nurse, who served on both sides during the war and has therefore a fair standard of comparison. Here are a few sentences from her reports:

'I have so often heard it said and repeated that the British soldiers are the dregs of London and the scum of the criminal classes, that their conduct astounded me.'

This is the opinion of a lady who spent two years in the service of humanity on the veldt.

Here are one or two other sidelights from Miss Bron:

'How grateful and respectful they all are! I go to the hospital at night without the slightest fear, and when a sentry hears my reply, "Sister," to his challenge, he always humbly begs my pardon.

'I have seen the last of them and their affectionate attentions, their respect, and their confidence. On this head I could relate many instances of exquisite feeling on the part of these poor soldiers.

'A wounded English soldier was speaking of Cronje. "Ah, sister," said he, "I am glad that we have made so many prisoners."

'"Why?" I asked, fearing to hear words of hatred.

'"Oh," he said, "I was glad to hear it because I know that they at least would be neither wounded nor killed. They will not leave wife nor children, neither will they suffer what we are suffering."'

She describes how she met General Wavell:

'"You see I have come to protect you," he said.

'We smiled and bowed, and I thought, "I know your soldiers too well, General. We don't need any protection."'

But war may have brutalised the combatants, and so it is of interest to have Nurse Bron's impressions at the end of 1901. She gives her conversation with a Boer:

'"All that I have to say to you is that what you did down there has never been seen in any other war. *Never* in any country in the world has such a dastardly act been committed as the shooting of one who goes to meet the white flag."

'Very pale, the chief, a true "gentleman" fifty-three years old, and the father of eleven children, answered, "You are right, sister."

'"And since we talk of these things," I said, "I will say that I understand very well that you are defending your country, but what I do not excuse is your lying as you do about these English."

'"We repeat what we are told."

'"No," I said, "you all of you lie, and you know that you are lying, with the Bible on your knees and invoking the name of God, and, thanks to your lies, all Europe believes that the English army is composed of assassins and thieves. You see how they treat you here!"'

She proceeds to show how they were treated. The patients, it may be observed, were not Boer combatants but Cape rebels, liable to instant execution. This is the diet after operations:

'For eight, or ten days, the patient has champagne *of the choicest French brands* (her italics), in considerable quantity, then old cognac, and finally port, stout, or ale at choice, with five or six eggs a day beaten up in brandy and milk, arriving at last at a complete diet of which I, though perfectly well, could not have absorbed the half.'

'This,' she says, 'is another instance of the "ferocity" with which, according to the European press, the English butchers have conducted the war.'

The Sisters of Nazareth in South Africa are a body who are above political or racial prejudice. Here are the published words of the Mother Superior:

'I receive letters by every mail, but a word that would imply the least shadow of reproach on the conduct of the soldiers has never been written. As for the British soldier in general, our sisters in various parts of the colony, who have come a great deal in contact with the military of all ranks, state that they can never say enough of their courtesy, politeness, and good behaviour at all times.'

These are not the impressions which the Boer agents, with their command of secret-service money and their influence on the European press, have given to the world. A constant stream of misrepresentations and lies have poisoned the mind of Europe and have made a deep and enduring breach between ourselves and our German kinsmen.

The British troops have been accused of shooting women. It is wonderful that many women have not been shot, for it has not been unusual for farmhouses to be defended by the men when there were women within. As a matter of fact, however, very few cases have occurred where a woman has been injured. One amazon was killed in the fighting line, rifle in hand, outside Ladysmith. A second victim furnished the famous Eloff myth, which gave material for many cartoons and editorials. The accusation was that in cold blood we had shot Kruger's niece, and a Berlin morning paper told the story, with many artistic embellishments, as follows:

'As the Boer saw his wife down, just able to raise herself, he made an attempt to run to her assistance, but the inhumans held him fast. The officer assured him that she was shot through the temples and must anyhow die, and they left her therefore lying. In the evening he heard his name called. It was his wife who still lived after twelve hours' agony. When they reached Rustenburg she was dead. This woman was Frau Eloff, Kruger's niece. In addition to the sympathy for the loss Kruger has suffered, this report will renew the bitter feeling of all against the brutality of English warfare.'

This story was dished up in many ways by many papers. Here is Lord Kitchener's plain account of the matter:

'No woman of that name has been killed, but the report may refer to the death of a Mrs. Vandermerve, who unfortunately was killed at a farmhouse from which her husband was firing. Mrs. Vandermerve is a sister-in-law of Eloff. The death of a woman from a stray bullet is greatly to be regretted, but it appears clear that her husband was responsible for the fighting which caused the accident.'

So perished another myth. I observe, however, now (Christmas 1901), a continental journalist describing an interview with Kruger says, 'he wore mourning on account of his niece who died of a gun-shot.' Might not his wife's death possibly account for the mourning?

And yet another invention which is destined to the same fate, is the story that at the skirmish of Graspan, near Reitz, upon June 6, the British used the Boer women as cover, a subject which also afforded excellent material for the caricaturists of the Fatherland. The picture of rows of charming Boer maidens chained in the open with bloodthirsty soldiers crouching behind them was too alluring for the tender-hearted artist. Nothing was wanting for a perfect cartoon—except the original fact. Here is the report as it appeared in a German paper:

'When the English on June 6 were attacked by the Boers, they ordered the women and children to leave the wagons. Placing these in front of the soldiers, they shot beneath the women's arms upon the approaching Boers. Eight women and two children fell through the Boers' fire. When the Boers saw this they stopped firing. Yelling like wild beasts, they broke through the soldiers' lines, beating to death the Tommies like mad dogs with the butt ends of their rifles.'

The true circumstances of the action so far as they can be collected are as follows: Early on June 6 Major Sladen, with 200 mounted infantry, ran down a Boer convoy of 100 wagons. He took forty-five male prisoners, and the wagons were full of women and children. He halted his men and waited for the main British force (De Lisle's) to come up. While he was waiting he was fiercely attacked by a large body of Boers, five or six hundred, under De Wet. The British threw themselves into a Kaffir kraal and made a desperate resistance. The long train of wagons with the women still in them extended from this village right across the plain, and the Boers used them as cover in skirmishing up to the village. The result was that the women and children were under a double fire from either side. One woman and two children appear to have been hit, though whether by Boer or Briton it must have been difficult to determine. The convoy and the prisoners remained eventually in the hands of the British. It will be seen then that it is as just to say that the Boers used their women as cover for their advance as the British for their defence. Probably in the heat of the action both sides thought more of the wagons than of what was inside them.

These, with one case at Middelburg, where in a night attack of the Boers one or two inmates of the refugee camp are said to have been accidentally hit, form the only known instances in the war. And yet so well known a paper as the German 'Kladderadatsch' is not ashamed to publish a picture of a ruined farm with dead women strewed round it, and the male child hanging from the branch of a tree. The 'Kladderadatsch' has a reputation as a comic paper, but there should be some limits to its facetiousness.

In his pamphlet on 'Methods of Barbarism,' Mr. Stead has recently produced a chapter called 'A Glimpse of the Hellish Panorama,' in which he deals with the evidence at the Spoelstra trial. Spoelstra was a Hollander who, having sworn an oath of neutrality, afterwards despatched a letter to a Dutch newspaper without submitting it to a censor, in which he made libellous attacks upon the British Army. He was tried for the offence and sentenced to a fine of 100£., his imprisonment being remitted. In the course of the trial he called a number of witnesses for the purpose of supporting his charges against the troops, and it is on their evidence that Mr. Stead dilates under the characteristic headline given above.

Mr. Stead begins his indictment by a paragraph which speaks for itself: 'It is a cant cry with many persons, by no means confined to those who have advocated the war, that the British Army has spent two years in the South African Republics without a single case of impropriety being proved against a single soldier. I should be very glad to believe it; but there is Rudyard Kipling's familiar saying that Tommy Atkins is no plaster saint, but a single man in barracks, or, in this case, a single man in camp, remarkably like other human beings. We all know him at home. There is not one father of a family in the House or on the London Press who would allow his servant girl to remain out all night on a public common in England in time of profound peace in the company of a score of soldiers. If he did, he would feel that he had exposed the girl to the loss of her character. This is not merely admitted, but acted upon by all decent people who live in garrison towns or in the neighbourhood of barracks. Why, then, should they suppose that when the same men are released from all the restraints of civilisation, and sent forth to burn, destroy, and loot at their own sweet will and pleasure, they will suddenly undergo so complete a transformation as to scrupulously respect the wives and daughters of the enemy? It is very unpopular to say this, and I already hear in advance the shrieks of execration of those who will declare that I am calumniating the gallant soldiers who are spending their lives in the defence of the interests of the Empire. But I do not say a word against our soldiers. I only say that they are men.'

He adds:

'It is an unpleasant fact, but it has got to be faced like other facts. No war can be conducted—and this war has not been conducted—without exposing multitudes of women, married and single, to the worst extremities of outrage. It is an inevitable incident of war. It is one of the normal phenomena of the military Inferno. It is absolutely impossible to attempt any comparative or quantitative estimate of the number of women who have suffered wrong at the hands of our troops.'

Was ever such an argument adduced in this world upon a serious matter! When stripped of its rhetoric it amounts to this, '250,000 men have committed outrages. How do I prove it? Because they are 250,000 men, and therefore *must* commit outrages.' Putting all chivalry, sense of duty, and every higher consideration upon one side, is Mr. Stead not aware that if a soldier had done such a thing and if his victim could have pointed him out, the man's life would be measured by the time that was needed to collect a military court to try him? Is there a soldier who does not know this? Is there a Boer who does not know it? It is the one offence for which there would be no possible forgiveness. Are the Boers so meek-spirited a race that they have no desire for vengeance? Would any officer take the responsibility of not reporting a man who was accused of such a crime? Where, then, are the lists of the men who must have suffered if this cruel accusation were true? There are no such lists, because such things have never occurred.

Leading up to the events of the trial, Mr. Stead curdles our blood by talking of the eleven women who stood up upon oath to testify to the ill- treatment which they had received at the hands of our troops. Taken with the context, the casual reader would naturally imagine that these eleven women were all complaining of some sexual ill-usage. In the very next sentence he talks about 'such horrible and shameful incidents.' But on examination it proves that eight out of the eleven cases have nothing sexual or, indeed, in many of them, anything criminal in their character. One is, that a coffin was dug up to see if there were arms in it. On this occasion the search was a failure, though it has before now been a success. Another was that the bed of a sick woman was searched—without any suggestion of indelicacy. Two others, that women had been confined while on the trek in wagons. 'The soldiers did not bother the woman during or after the confinement. They did not peep into the wagon,' said the witness. These are the trivialities which Mr. Stead tries to bluff us into classifying as 'horrible and shameful incidents.'

But there were three alleged cases of assault upon women. One of them is laid to the charge of a certain Mr. E——n, of the Intelligence Department. Now, the use of Mr. and the description 'Intelligence Department' make it very doubtful whether this man could be called a member of the British Army at all. The inference is that he was a civilian, and further, that he was a Dutch civilian. British names which will fit E——n are not common, while the Dutch name Esselen or Enslin is extremely so. 'I have never been to the Intelligence Department to find out whether he really belonged to that Department,' said the woman. She adds that E——n acted as an interpreter. Surely, then, he must have been a Dutchman. In that case, why is his name the only name which is disguised? Is it not a little suggestive?

The second case was that of Mrs. Gouws, whose unfortunate experience was communicated to Pastor van Broekhuizen, and had such an effect upon him as to cause him to declare that 30 per cent of the women of the country had been ruined. Mrs. Gouws certainly appears by her own account to have been very roughly treated, though she does not assert that her assailant went to the last extremity—or, indeed, that he did more than use coarse terms in his conversation. The husband in his evidence says: 'I have seen a great deal of soldiers, and they behaved well, and I could speak well of them.' He added that a British officer had taken his wife's deposition, and that both the Provost-Marshal and the Military Governor were interesting themselves in the case. Though no actual assault was committed, it is to be hoped that the man who was rude to a helpless woman will sooner or later be identified and punished.

There remains one case, that of Mrs. Botha of Rustenburg, which, if her account is corroborated, is as bad as it could be. The mystery of the case lies in the fact that by her own account a British force was encamped close by, and yet that neither she nor her husband made the complaint which would have brought most summary punishment upon the criminal. This could not have been from a shrinking from publicity, since she was ready to tell the story in Court. There is not the least indication who this solitary soldier may have been, and even the date was unknown to the complainant. What can be done in such a case? The President of the court-martial, with a burst of indignation which shows that he at least does not share Mr. Stead's views upon the frequency of such crimes in South Africa, cried: 'If such a most awful thing happened to a woman, would it not be the first thing for a man to do to rush out and bring the guilty man to justice? He ought to risk his life for that. There was no reason for him to be frightened. We English are not a barbarous nation.' The husband, however, had taken no steps. We may be very sure that the case still engages the earnest attention of our Provost-Marshal, and that the man, if he exists, will sooner or later form an object-lesson upon discipline and humanity to the nearest garrison. Such was the Spoelstra trial. Mr. Stead talks fluently of the charges made, but deliberately omits the essential fact that after a patient hearing not one of them was substantiated.

I cannot end the chapter better than with the words of the Rev. P. S. Bosman, head of the Dutch Reformed Church at Pretoria:

'Not a single case of criminal assault or rape by non-commissioned officers or men of the British Army in Pretoria on Boer women has come to my knowledge. I asked several gentlemen in turn about this point and their testimony is the same as mine.'

But Mr. Stead says that it must be so because there are 250,000 men in Africa. Could the perversion of argument go further? Which are we to believe, our enemy upon the spot or the journalist in London?

IX. FURTHER CHARGES AGAINST BRITISH TROOPS

Expansive and Explosive Bullets.

When Mr. Stead indulges in vague rhetoric it is difficult to corner him, but when he commits himself to a definite statement he is more open to attack. Thus, in his 'Methods of Barbarism' he roundly asserts that 'England sent several million rounds of expanding bullets to South Africa, and in the North of the Transvaal and at Mafeking for the first three months of the war no other bullets were used.' Mr. Methuen, on the authority of a letter of Lieutenant de Montmorency, R.A., states also that from October 12, 1899, up to January 15, 1900, the British forces north of Mafeking used nothing but Mark IV. ammunition, which is not a dum-dum but is an expansive bullet.

Mr. Methuen's statement differs, as will be seen, very widely from Mr. Stead's; for Mr. Stead says Mafeking, and Mr. Methuen says north of Mafeking. There was a very great deal of fighting at Mafeking, and comparatively little north of Mafeking during that time, so that the difference is an essential one. To test Mr. Stead's assertion about Mafeking, I communicated with General Baden-Powell, the gentleman who is most qualified to speak as to what occurred there, and his answer lies before me: 'We had no expanding bullets in our supply at Mafeking, unless you call the ordinary Martini-Henry an expanding bullet. I would not have used them on humane principles, and moreover, an Army order had been issued against the use of dum-dum bullets in this campaign. On the other hand, explosive bullets are expressly forbidden in the Convention, and these the Boers used freely against us in Mafeking, especially on May 12.'

I have endeavoured also to test the statement as it concerns the troops to the north of Mafeking. The same high authority says: 'With regard to the northern force, it is just possible that a few sportsmen in the Rhodesian column may have had some sporting bullets, but I certainly never heard of them.' A friend of mine who was in Lobatsi during the first week of the war assures me that he never saw anything but the solid bullet. It must be remembered that the state of things was very exceptional with the Rhodesian force. Their communications to the south were cut on the second day of the war, and for seven months they were dependent upon the long and circuitous Beira route for any supplies which reached them. One could imagine that under such circumstances uniformity of armament would be more difficult to maintain than in the case of an army with an assured base.

The expansive bullet is not, as a matter of fact, contrary to the Conventions of The Hague. It was expressly held from being so by the representatives of the United States and of Great Britain. In taking this view I cannot but think that these two enlightened and humanitarian Powers were ill-advised. Those Conventions were of course only binding on those who signed them, and therefore in fighting desperate savages the man-stopping bullet could still have been used. Whatever our motives in taking the view that we did, a swift retribution has come upon us, for it has prevented us from exacting any retribution, or even complaining, when the Boers have used these weapons against us. Explosive bullets are, however, as my distinguished correspondent points out, upon a different footing, and if the Boers claim the advantages of the Conventions of The Hague, then every burgher found with these weapons in his bandolier is liable to punishment.

Our soldiers have been more merciful than our Hague diplomatists, for in spite of the reservation of the right to use this ammunition, every effort has been made to exclude it from the firing line. An unfortunate incident early in the campaign gave our enemies some reason to suspect us. The facts are these.

At the end of the spring of 1899 some hundreds of thousands of hollow- headed bullets, made in England, were condemned as unsatisfactory, not being true to gauge, &c., and were sent to South Africa for target practice only. A quantity of this ammunition, known as 'Metford Mark IV.,' was sent up to Dundee by order of General Symons for practice in field firing. As Mark IV. was not for use in a war with white races all these cartridges were called in as soon as Kruger declared war, and the officers responsible thought they were everyone returned. By some blundering in the packing at home, however, some of this Mark IV. must have got mixed up with the ordinary, or Mark II., ammunition, and was found on our men by the Boers on October 30. Accordingly a very careful inspection was ordered, and a few Mark IV. bullets were found in our men's pouches, and at once removed. Their presence was purely accidental, and undoubtedly caused by a blunder in the Ordnance Department long before the war, and it was in consequence of this that some hollow-headed bullets were fired by the English early in the war without their knowledge.

What is usually known as the dum-dum bullet is a 'soft-nosed' one: but the regulation Mark II. is also made at the dum-dum factory, and the Boers, seeing the dum-dum label on boxes containing the latter, naturally thought the contents were the soft-nosed, which they were not.

It must be admitted that there was some carelessness in permitting sporting ammunition ever to get to the front at all. When the Derbyshire Militia were taken by De Wet at Roodeval, a number of cases of sporting cartridges were captured by the Boers (the officers had used them for shooting springbok). My friend, Mr. Langman, who was present, saw the Boers, in some instances, filling their bandoliers from these cases on the plausible excuse that they were only using our own ammunition. Such cartridges should never have been permitted to go up. But in spite of instances of bungling, the evidence shows that every effort has been made to keep the war as humane as possible. I am inclined to hope that a fuller knowledge will show that the same holds good for our enemies, and that in spite of individual exceptions, they have never systematically used anything except what one of their number described as a 'gentlemanly' bullet.

Conduct to Prisoners on the Field.

On this count, also, the British soldiers have been exposed to attacks, both at home and abroad, which are as unfounded and as shameful as most of those which have been already treated.

The first occasion upon which Boer prisoners fell into our hands was at the Battle of Elandslaagte, on October 21, 1899. That night was spent by the victorious troops in a pouring rain, round such fires as they were able to light. It has been recorded by several witnesses that the warmest corner by the fire was reserved for the Boer prisoners. It has been asserted, and is again asserted, that when the Lancers charged a small body of the enemy after the action, they gave no quarter—'too well substantiated and too familiar,' says one critic of this assertion. I believe, as a matter of fact, that the myth arose from a sensational picture in an illustrated paper. The charge was delivered late in the evening, in uncertain light. Under such circumstances it is always possible, amid so wild and confused a scene, that a man who would have surrendered has been cut down or ridden over. But the cavalry brought back twenty prisoners, and the number whom they killed or wounded has not been placed higher than that, so that it is certain there was no indiscriminate slaying. I have read a letter from the officer who commanded the cavalry and who directed the charge, in which he tells the whole story confidentially to a brother officer. He speaks of his prisoners, but there is no reference to any brutality upon the part of the troopers.

Mr. Stead makes a great deal of some extracts from the letters of private soldiers at the front who talk of bayoneting their enemies. Such expressions should be accepted with considerable caution, for it may amuse the soldier to depict himself as rather a terrible fellow to his home-staying friends. Even if isolated instances could be corroborated, it would merely show that men of fiery temperament in the flush of battle are occasionally not to be restrained, either by the power of discipline or by the example and exhortations of their officers. Such instances, I do not doubt, could be found among all troops in all wars. But to found upon it a general charge of brutality or cruelty is unjust in the case of a foreigner, and unnatural in the case of our own people.

There is one final and complete answer to all such charges. It is that we have now in our hands 42,000 males of the Boer nations. They assert, and we cannot deny, that their losses in killed have been extraordinarily light during two years of warfare. How are these admitted and certain facts compatible with any general refusal of quarter? To anyone who, like myself, has seen the British soldiers jesting and smoking cigarettes with their captives within five minutes of their being taken, such a charge is ludicrous, but surely even to the most biased mind the fact stated above must be conclusive.

In some ways I fear that the Conventions of The Hague will prove, when tested on a large scale, to be a counsel of perfection. It will certainly be the extreme test of self-restraint and discipline—a test successfully endured by the British troops at Elandslaagte, Bergendal, and many other places—to carry a position by assault and then to give quarter to those defenders who only surrender at the last instant. It seems almost too much to ask. The assailants have been terribly punished: they have lost their friends and their officers, in the frenzy of battle they storm the position, and then at the last instant the men who have done all the mischief stand up unscathed from behind their rocks and claim their own personal safety. Only at that moment has the soldier seen his antagonist or been on equal terms with him. He must give quarter, but it must be confessed that this is trying human nature rather high.

But if this holds good of an organised force defending a position, how about the solitary sniper? The position of such a man has never been defined by the Conventions of The Hague, and no rules are laid down for his treatment. It is not wonderful if the troops who have been annoyed by him should on occasion take the law into their own hands and treat him in a summary fashion.

The very first article of the Conventions of The Hague states that a belligerent must (1) Be commanded by some responsible person; (2) Have a distinctive emblem visible at a distance; (3) Carry arms openly. Now it is evident that the Boer sniper who draws his Mauser from its hiding-place in order to have a shot at the Rooineks from a safe kopje does not comply with any one of these conditions. In the letter of the law, then, he is undoubtedly outside the rules of warfare.

In the spirit he is even more so. Prowling among the rocks and shooting those who cannot tell whence the bullet comes, there is no wide gap between him and the assassin. His victims never see him, and in the ordinary course he incurs no personal danger. I believe such cases to have been very rare, but if the soldiers have occasionally shot such a man without reference to the officers, can it be said that it was an inexcusable action, or even that it was outside the strict rules of warfare?

I find in the 'Gazette de Lausanne' a returned Swiss soldier named Pache, who had fought for the Boers, expresses his amazement at the way in which the British troops after their losses in the storming of a position gave quarter to those who had inflicted those losses upon them.

'Only once,' he says, 'at the fight at Tabaksberg, have I seen the Boers hold on to their position to the very end. At the last rush of the enemy they opened a fruitless magazine fire, and then threw down their rifles and lifted their hands, imploring quarter from those whom they had been firing at at short range. I was astounded at the clemency of the soldiers, who allowed them to live. For my part I should have put them to death.'

Of prisoners after capture there is hardly need to speak. There is a universal consensus of opinion from all, British or foreign, who have had an opportunity of forming an opinion, that the prisoners have been treated with humanity and generosity. The same report has come from Green Point, St. Helena, Bermuda, Ceylon, Ahmednager, and all other camps. An outcry was raised when Ahmednager in India was chosen for a prison station, and it was asserted, with that recklessness with which so many other charges have been hurled against the authorities, that it was a hot-bed of disease. Experience has shown that there was no grain of truth in these statements, and the camp has been a very healthy one. As it remains the only one which has ever been subjected to harsh criticism, it may be of use to append the conclusions of Mr. Jesse Collings during a visit to it last month:

'The Boer officers said, speaking for ourselves and men, we have nothing at all to complain of. As prisoners of war we could not be better treated, and Major Dickenson' (this they wished specially to be inserted), 'is as kind and considerate as it is possible to be.'

Some sensational statements were also made in America as to the condition of the Bermuda Camps, but a newspaper investigation has shown that there is no charge to be brought against them.

Mr. John J. O'Rorke writes to the 'New York Times,' saying, 'That in view of the many misrepresentations regarding the treatment of the Boer prisoners in Bermuda, he recently obtained a trustworthy opinion from one of his correspondents there.'... The correspondent's name is Musson Wainwright, and Mr. O'Rorke describes him 'as one of the influential residents in the island.' He says, 'That the Boers in Bermuda are better off than many residents in New York. They have plenty of beef, plenty of bread, plenty of everything except liberty. There are good hospitals and good doctors. It is true that some of the Boers are short of clothing, but these are very few, and the Government is issuing clothing to them. On the whole,' says Mr. Wainwright, 'Great Britain is treating the Boers far better than most people would.'

Compare this record with the undoubted privations, many of them unnecessary, which our soldiers endured at Waterval near Pretoria, the callous neglect of the enteric patients there, and the really barbarous treatment of British Colonial prisoners who were confined in cells on the absurd plea that in fighting for their flag they were traitors to the Africander cause.

Executions.

The number of executions of Boers, as distinguished from the execution of Cape rebels, has been remarkably few in a war which has already lasted twenty-six months. So far as I have been able to follow them, they have been limited to the execution of Cordua for broken parole and conspiracy upon August 24, 1900, at Pretoria, the shooting of one or two horse-poisoners in Natal, and the shooting of three men after the action of October 27, 1900, near Fredericstad. These men, after throwing down their arms and receiving quarter, picked them up again and fired at the soldiers from behind. No doubt there have been other cases, scattered up and down the vast scene of warfare, but I can find no record of them, and if they exist at all they must be few in number. Since the beginning of 1901 four men have been shot in the Transvaal, three in Pretoria as spies and breakers of parole, one in Johannesburg as an aggravated case of breaking neutrality by inciting Boers to resist.

At the beginning of the war 90 per cent. of the farmers in the northern district of Cape Colony joined the invaders. Upon the expulsion of the Boers these men for the most part surrendered. The British Government, recognising that pressure had been put upon them and that their position had been a difficult one, inflicted no penalty upon the rank-and-file beyond depriving them of the franchise for a few years. A few who, like the Douglas rebels, were taken red-handed upon the field of battle, were condemned to periods of imprisonment which varied from one to five years.

This was in the year 1900. In 1901 there was an invasion of the Colony by Boers which differed very much from the former one. In the first case the country had actually been occupied by the Boer forces, who were able to exert real pressure upon the inhabitants. In the second the invaders were merely raiding bands who traversed many places but occupied none. A British subject who joined on the first occasion might plead compulsion, on the second it was undoubtedly of his own free will.

These Boer bands being very mobile, and never fighting save when they were at an overwhelming advantage, penetrated all parts of the Colony and seduced a number of British subjects from their allegiance. The attacking of small posts and the derailing of trains, military or civilian, were their chief employment. To cover their tracks they continually murdered natives whose information might betray them. Their presence kept the Colony in confusion and threatened the communications of the Army.

The situation may be brought home to a continental reader by a fairly exact parallel. Suppose that an Austrian army had invaded Germany, and that while it was deep in German territory bands of Austrian subjects who were of German extraction began to tear up the railway lines and harass the communications. That was our situation in South Africa. Would the Austrians under these circumstances show much mercy to those rebel bands, especially if they added cold-blooded murder to their treason? Is it likely that they would?

The British, however, were very long-suffering. Many hundreds of these rebels passed into their hands, and most of them escaped with fine and imprisonment. The ringleaders, and those who were convicted of capital penal offences, were put to death. I have been at some pains to make a list of the executions in 1901, including those already mentioned. It is at least approximately correct:

Number	Place	Date	Reason
		1901	
2	De Aar	March 19	Train wrecking.
2	Pretoria	June 11	Boers breaking oath of neutrality.
1	Middelburg	July 10	Fighting.
1	Cape Town........	" 13	"
1	Cradock...	" 13	"
2	Middelburg.......	" 24	"
2	Kenhardt	" 25	"
1	Pretoria..........	Aug. 22	Boer spy.
3	Colesburg.	Sept. 4	Fighting.
1	Middelburg.	Oct. 10	"
1	Middelburg.	" 11	"
1	Vryburg (hanged).	" 12	"
Several	Tarkastad........	" 12	"
1	Tarkastad........	" 14	"
1	Middelburg	" 15	"
2	Cradock (1 hanged, 1 shot)..........	" 17	Train-wrecking and murdering native.
2	Vryburg	" 29	Fighting.
1	Mafeking.........	Nov. 11	Shooting a native.
1	Colesburg	" 12	Fighting, marauding, and assaulting, etc.
1	Johannesburg	" 23	Persuading surrendered burghers to break oath.
1	Aliwal North.....	" 26	Cape Police deserter.
1	Krugersdorp......	Dec. 26	Shooting wounded.
2	Mafeking.........	" 27	Kaffir murder.

Allowing 3 for the 'several' at Tarkastad on October 12, that makes a total of 34. Many will undoubtedly be added in the future, for the continual murder of inoffensive natives, some of them children, calls for stern justice. In this list 4 were train-wreckers (aggravated cases by rebels), 1 was a spy, 4 were murderers of natives, 1 a deserter who took twenty horses from the Cape Police, and the remaining 23 were British subjects taken fighting and bearing arms against their own country.

Hostages upon Railway Trains.

Here the military authorities are open, as it seems to me, to a serious charge, not of inhumanity to the enemy but of neglecting those steps which it was their duty to take in order to safeguard their own troops. If all the victims of derailings and railway cuttings were added together it is not an exaggeration to say that it would furnish as many killed and wounded as a considerable battle. On at least five occasions between twenty and thirty men were incapacitated, and there are very numerous cases where smaller numbers were badly hurt.

Let it be said at once that we have no grievance in this. To derail a train is legitimate warfare, with many precedents to support it. But to checkmate it by putting hostages upon the trains is likewise legitimate warfare, with many precedents to support it also. The Germans habitually did it in France, and the result justified them as the result has justified us. From the time (October 1901) that it was adopted in South Africa we have not heard of a single case of derailing, and there can be no doubt that the lives of many soldiers, and possibly of some civilians, have been saved by the measure.

I will conclude this chapter by two extracts chosen out of many from the diary of the Austrian, Count Sternberg. In the first he describes his capture:

'Three hours passed thus without our succeeding in finding our object. The sergeant then ordered that we should take a rest. We sat down on the ground, and chatted good-humouredly with the soldiers. They were fine fellows, without the least sign of brutality—in fact, full of sympathy. They had every right to be angry with us, for we had spoiled their sleep after they had gone through a trying day; yet they did not visit it on us in any way, and were most kind. They even shared their drinking-water with us. I cannot describe what my feelings were that night. A prisoner!'

He adds: 'I can only repeat that the English officers and the English soldiers have shown in this war that the profession of arms does not debase, but rather ennobles man.'

X. THE OTHER SIDE OF THE QUESTION

Writing in November 1900, after hearing an expression of opinion from many officers from various parts of the seat of war, I stated in 'The Great Boer War': 'The Boers have been the victims of a great deal of cheap slander in the press. The men who have seen most of the Boers in the field are the most generous in estimating their character. That the white flag was hoisted by the Boers as a cold-blooded device for luring our men into the open, is an absolute calumny. To discredit their valour is to discredit our victory.' My own opinion would have been worthless, but this was, as I say, the result of considerable inquiry. General Porter said: 'On a few occasions the white flag was abused, but in what large community would you not find a few miscreants?' General Lyttelton said: 'The Boers are brave men, and I do not think that the atrocities which have been reported are the acts of the regular Dutch burghers, but of the riff-raff who get into all armies.'

It is a painful fact, but the words could not possibly be written to-day. Had the war only ended when it should have ended, the combatants might have separated each with a chivalrous feeling of respect for a knightly antagonist. But the Boers having appealed to the God of battles and heard the judgment, appealed once more against it. Hence came the long, bitter, and fruitless struggle which has cost so many lives, so much suffering, and a lowering of the whole character of the war.

It is true that during the first year there were many things to exasperate the troops. The Boers were a nation of hunters and they used many a ruse which seemed to the straightforward soldier to be cowardly and unfair. Individuals undoubtedly played the white-flag trick, and individuals were guilty of holding up their hands in order to lure the soldiers from their cover. There are many instances of this—indeed, in one case Lord Roberts was himself a witness of it. Appended is his official protest:

'Another instance having occurred of a gross abuse of the white flag and of the signal of holding up the hands in token of surrender, it is my duty to inform your Honour that if such abuse occurs again I shall most reluctantly be compelled to order my troops to disregard the white flag entirely.

'The instance occurred on the kopje east of Driefontein Farm yesterday evening, and was witnessed by several of my own staff officers, as well as by myself, and resulted in the wounding of several of my officers and men.

'A large quantity of explosive bullets of three different kinds was found in Cronje's laager, and after every engagement with your Honour's troops.

'Such breaches of the recognised usages of war and of the Geneva Convention are a disgrace to any civilised power.'

But British officers were not unreasonable. They understood that they were fighting against a force in which the individual was a law unto himself. It was not fair to impute to deliberate treachery upon the part of the leaders every slim trick of an unscrupulous burgher. Again, it was understood that a coward may hoist an unauthorised white flag and his braver companions may refuse to recognise it, as our own people might on more than one occasion have done with advantage. For these reasons there was very little bitterness against the enemy, and most officers would, I believe, have subscribed the opinion which I have expressed.

From the first the position of the Boers was entirely irregular as regards the recognised rules of warfare. The first article of the Conventions of The Hague insists that an army in order to claim belligerent rights must first wear some emblem which is visible at a distance. It is true that the second article is to the effect that a population which has no time to organise themselves and who are defending themselves may be excused from this rule; but the Boers were the invaders at the outset of the war, and in view of their long and elaborate preparations it is absurd to say that they could not have furnished burghers on commando with some distinctive badge. When they made a change it was for the worse, for they finally dressed themselves in the khaki uniforms of our own soldiers, and by this means effected several surprises. It is typical of the good humour of the British that very many of these khaki-clad burghers have passed through our hands, and that no penalty has ever been inflicted upon them for their dangerous breach of the rules of war. In this, as in the case of the train hostages, we have gone too far in the direction of clemency. Had the first six khaki-clad burghers been shot, the lives of many of our soldiers would have been saved.

The question of uniform was condoned, however, just as the white-flag incidents were condoned. We made allowance for the peculiarities of the warfare, and for the difficulties of our enemies. We tried to think that they were playing the game as fairly as they could. Already their methods were certainly rough. Here, for example, is a sworn narrative of a soldier taken in the fighting before Ladysmith:

'Evidence of No. 6418 Private F. Ayling, 3rd Batt. King's Royal Rifles.

'Near Colenso, February 25, 1900.

'I was taken prisoner about 5 A.M. on 23rd instant by the Boers, being too far in front of my company to retire. I was allowed to go about 10 A.M. on the 25th, and rejoined my regiment.

'During this time I was kept in the Boer trenches without food or drink. There were quite twenty of our wounded lying close to the trenches, and asking for water all the time, which was always refused. If any of the wounded moved they were shot at. Most of them died for want of assistance, as they were lying there two days and two nights. The Boers (who seemed to be all English) said, "Let them die, and give them no water."'

Such instances may, however, be balanced against others where kind- hearted burghers have shown commiseration and generosity to our wounded and prisoners.

As the war dragged on, however, it took a more savage character upon the part of our enemy, and it says much for the discipline of the British troops that they have held their hands and refused to punish a whole nation for the cruelty and treachery of a few. The first absolute murder in the war was that of Lieutenant Neumeyer, which occurred at the end of November 1900. The facts, which have since been officially confirmed, were thus reported at the time from Aliwal:

'Lieutenant Neumeyer, commanding the Orange River Police at Smithfield, was driving here, unarmed, in a cart yesterday, when he was "held up" by two Boers. He was taken prisoner, handcuffed, and treacherously shot in the back with a revolver and again through the head.

'The murderers stripped off the leggings which Lieutenant Neumeyer was wearing, searched his clothes for money, and afterwards dragged the body to a sluit, where, later in the day it was discovered by the Cape Police and brought here. Two natives were eye-witnesses of the murder. Lieutenant Neumeyer had served with distinction in the Rhodesian campaign.'

At this latter period of the war began that systematic murdering of the Kaffirs by the Boers which has been the most savage and terrible feature in the whole business. On both sides Kaffirs have been used as teamsters, servants, and scouts, but on neither side as soldiers. The British could with the greatest ease have swamped the whole Boer resistance at the beginning of the war by letting loose the Basutos, the Zulus, and the Swazis, all of whom have blood-feuds with the Boers. It is very certain that the Boers would have had no such compunctions, for when in 1857 the Transvaalers had a quarrel with the Free State we have Paul Botha's evidence for the fact that they intrigued with a Kaffir chief to attack their kinsmen from the rear. Botha says:

'I have particular knowledge of this matter, because I took part in the commando which our Government sent to meet the Transvaal forces. The dispute was eventually amicably settled, but, incredible as it may seem, the Transvaal had actually sent five persons, headed by the notorious Karel Geere, to Moshesh, the Basuto chief, to prevail upon him to attack *us*, their kinsmen, in the rear! I was one of the patrol that captured Geere and his companions, some of whom I got to know subsequently, and who revealed to me the whole dastardly plot.'

This will give some idea as to what we might have had to expect had native sympathy gone the other way. In the letter already quoted, written by Snyman to his brother, he asserts that Kruger told him that he relied upon the assistance of the Swazis and Zulus. As it was, however, beyond allowing natives to defend their own lives and property when attacked, as in the case of the Baralongs at Mafeking, and the Kaffirs in the Transkei, we have only employed Kaffirs in the pages of the continental cartoons.

As teamsters, servants, guides, and scouts the Kaffirs were, however, essential to us, and realising this the Boers, when the war began to go against them, tried to terrorise them into deserting us by killing them without mercy whenever they could in any way connect them with the British. How many hundreds were done to death in this fashion it is impossible to compute. After a British defeat no mercy was shown to the drivers of the wagons and the native servants. Boer commandos covered their tracks by putting to death every Kaffir who might give information. Sometimes they killed even the children. Thus Lord Kitchener, in his report, narrates a case where a British column hard upon the track of a Boer commando found four little Kaffir boys with their brains dashed out in the kraal which the Boers had just evacuated.

A case which particularly touched the feelings of the British people was that of Esau, the coloured blacksmith, who was a man of intelligence and education, living as a loyal British subject in the British town of Calvinia. There was no possible case of 'spying' here, since the man had not left his own town. The appended documents will show why the nation will not have done its duty until justice has been done upon the murderers. A touching letter has been published from Esau to the governor of the district in which he says that, come what may, he would be loyal to the flag under which he was born. The next news of him was of his brutal murder:

'Abraham Esau, a loyal coloured blacksmith, was mercilessly flogged for refusing to give information as to where arms were buried. Inflammation of the kidneys set in; nevertheless he was again beaten through the village with sjamboks until he was unable to walk, and was then shot dead.'—Calvinia, February 8. ('Times,' February 16, 1901, p. 7 [3]).

'The district surgeon at Calvinia, writing to the Colonial secretary, has fully confirmed the flogging and shooting of Esau by a Boer named Strydom, who stated that he acted in accordance with orders. No trial was held, and no reason is alleged for the deed.'—Cape Town, February 19. ('Times,' February 20, 1901, p. 5 [3]).

'The authority for the statement of the flogging by the Boers of a coloured man named Esau at Calvinia was a Reuter's telegram, confirmed subsequently by the report made to Cape Town by the district surgeon of Calvinia.'—From Mr. Brodrick's reply to Mr. Labouchere in House of Commons, February 21. ('Times,' February 22, 1901).

'I had a telegram from Sir A. Milner in confirmation of the reports from various quarters that have reached me. The High Commissioner states that the name of the district surgeon who reported the mal-treatment of the coloured man is Foote. Sir A. Milner adds: "There is absolutely no doubt about the murder of Esau."'—From Mr. Brodrick's reply to Mr. Dillon in House of Commons, February 22. ('Times,' February 23, 1901).

The original rule of the British Service was that the black scouts should be unarmed, so as to avoid all accusations of arming natives. When it was found that they were systematically shot they were given rifles, as it was inhuman to expose them to death without any means of defence. I believe that some armed Kaffirs who watch the railway line have also been employed in later phases of the war, the weapons to be used in self-defence. Considering how pressed the British were at one time, and considering that by a word they could have thrown a large and highly disciplined Indian army into the scales, I think that their refusal to do so is one of the most remarkable examples of moderation in history. The French had no hesitation in using Turcos against the Germans, nor did the Americans refrain from using Negro regiments against the Spaniards. We made it a white man's war, however, and I think that we did wisely and well.

So far did the Boers carry their murderous tactics against the natives, that British prisoners with dark complexions were in imminent danger. Thus at a skirmish at Doorn River on July 27, 1901, the seven Kaffir scouts taken with the British were shot in cold blood, and an Englishman named Finch was shot with them in the alleged belief that he had Kaffir blood. Here is the evidence of the latter murder:

No. 28284 Trooper Charles Catton, 22nd Imperial Yeomanry, being duly sworn, states:

'At Doorn River on 27th July, 1901, I was one of the patrol captured by the Boers, and after we had surrendered I saw a man lying on the ground, wounded, between two natives. I saw a Boer go up to him and shoot him through the chest. I noticed the man, Trooper Finch, was alive. I do not know the name of the Boer who shot him, but I could recognise him again.'

No. 33966 Trooper F. W. Madams, having been duly sworn, states:

'I was one of the patrol captured by the Boers on 27th July, 1901, near Doorn River. After we had surrendered I went to look for my hat, and after finding it I was passing the wounded man, Trooper Finch, when I saw a Boer, whose name I do not know, shoot Trooper Finch through the chest with a revolver. I could identify the man who shot him.'

This scandal of the murder of the Kaffirs, a scandal against which no protest seems to have been raised by the pro-Boer press in England or the Continent, has reached terrible proportions. I append some of the evidence from recent official reports from the front:

Case at Magaliesberg.—About October or November 1900, the bodies of nine natives were found lying together on the top of the Magaliesberg. Of these five were intelligence natives, the remainder being boys employed by the Boers, but suspected of giving information. The witnesses in this case are now difficult to find, as they are all natives; but it appears that the natives were tried by an informal court, of which B. A. Klopper, ex-President of the Volksraad, was president, and condemned to death. Hendrik Schoeman, son of the late general, and Piet Joubert are reported to have acted as escort.

Case of five natives murdered near Wilge River.—On capturing a train near Wilge River, Transvaal, on March 11, 1901, the Boers took five unarmed natives on one side and shot them, throwing their bodies into a ditch. Corporal Sutton, of the Hampshire Regiment, saw, after the surrender, a Boer put five shots into a native who was lying down. Other soldiers on the train vouch to seeing one man deliberately shoot five boys in cold blood.

Case of eight Kaffir boys.—On or about July 17, 1901, eight Kaffir boys, between the ages of twelve and fourteen, went out from Uitkijk, near Edenburg, to get oranges. None were armed. Boers opened fire, shot one, captured six; one escaped, and is now with Major Damant. Corporal Willett, Damant's Horse, afterwards saw boys' bodies near farm, but so disfigured that they could not be recognised. Some Kaffirs were then sent out from Edenburg and recognised them. One boy is supposed to have been spared by Boers, body not found. Lieutenant Kentish, Royal Irish Fusiliers, saw bodies, and substantially confirms murder, and states Boers were under Field-Cornet Dutoit.

Case of Klass, Langspruit, Standerton.—Klass's wife states that on August 3, 1901, Cornelius Laas, of Langspruit, and another Boer came to the kraal and told Klass to go with them. On his demurring they accused him of giving information to the British, and C. Laas shot him through the back of the head as he ran away. Another native, the wife of a native clergyman at Standerton, saw the dead body.

Case of Two Natives near Hopetown.—On August 22, 1901, Private C. P. Fivaz, of the Cape Mounted Police, along with two natives, was captured near Venter Hoek, Hopetown district, by a force under Commandant Van Reenan. He had off-saddled at the time, and the natives were sleeping in a stable. He heard Van Reenan give his men an order to shoot the natives, which order was promptly carried out in his presence as regards one man, and he was told that the other had also been shot. The resident on the farm, A. G. Liebenberg, who warned Fivaz at 5 A.M. of the approach of the enemy, buried both the bodies where he found them— viz., one about forty yards from the house and the other about five hundred yards away. His statement is corroborated by his son, who saw one of the boys killed.

Case of John Makran.—John Makran and Alfius Bampa (the witness) are unarmed natives living near Warmbaths, north of Pretoria. On the evening of September 17, 1901, Andries

Van der Walt and a party of Boers surrounded Makran's house. Van der Walt told the boy to come out, and when he did so two men seized him. While two men held Makran's hands up Van der Walt stood five yards behind him and shot him through the head with a Mauser rifle. When the boy fell he shot him again through the heart, and then with a knife cut a deep gash across his forehead. Both these boys formerly worked for Van der Walt.

Case at Zandspruit.—On the night of October 1, 1901, about 11.30 P.M., a party of Boers surrounded a native house at Dassie Klip, near Zandspruit, and killed four natives in or about the house. The party consisted of twenty-four, under the following leaders: Dirk Badenhorst, of Dassie Klip; Cornelius Erasmus, of Streepfontein; and C. Van der Merwe, of Rooi Draai. The witnesses in this case are all natives residing at Dassie Klip, who knew the assailants well. In one case a native called Karle was endeavouring to escape over a wall, but was wounded in the thigh. On seeing he was not dead, Stoffel Visagie, of Skuilhoek, drew a revolver and shot him through the head. The charge against these natives appears to have been that they harboured British scouts.

Case of Jim Zulu.—On or about October 18, 1901, V. C. Thys Pretorius (presumably of Pretoria), with seventy men, visited Waterval North, on the Pretoria-Pietersburg line, and practically murdered two natives, wounding three others, one of whom afterwards died. The witnesses state that on the morning of October 18, 1901, Pretorius came to a colliery near Waterval North and called for Jim Zulu, and on his appearance shot him through the face. Three days later this native died of his wounds. At the same time he and another man, named Dorsehasmus, also shot three other natives.

Here is a further list, showing how systematic has been this brutality. I reproduce it in its official curtness:

Report of Resident Magistrate, Barkly West, January 28, 1900.—Native despatch rider shot and mutilated.

November or December 1900.—Near Virginia two natives were shot, being accused of showing the British the road to Ventersburg.

Report of Resident Magistrate, Taungs, December 4, 1900.—Three natives murdered at Border Siding.

December 18, 1900.—Native, Philip, shot at Vlakplaats, eight miles south-west of Pretoria, by J. Johnson and J. Dilmar, of J. Joubert's commando.

Report of Resident Magistrate, Taungs, December 24, 1900.—Native shot by Boers at Pudimoe. Three natives killed at Christiana.

Report of Resident Magistrate, Herschel, January 6, 1901.— Two natives shot as spies.

Report of Resident Magistrate, Calvinia, January 29, 1901.—Esau case and ill-treatment of other natives.

February 28, 1901.—Zulu boy shot dead at Zevenfontein, between Pretoria and Johannesburg, charged with giving information to the British, by men of Field-Cornet Jan Joubert's commando.

Report of Resident Magistrate, Cradock, March 21, 1901.— Murder of native witness, Salmon Booi.

Report of Resident Magistrate, Taungs, May 8, 1901.— Natives shot by Boers at Manthe.

Report of Resident Magistrate, Gordonia, May 23, 1901.—
Native shot dead.

May 25, 1901.—District Harrismith. A native accused of
laziness and insolence was shot by men in M. Prinsloo's
commando.

May 28, 1901.—At Sannah's Post three natives were
captured and shot.

June 5, 1901.—Three natives with Colonel Plumer's column
captured and shot near Paardeberg.

July 27, 1901.—Seven natives captured with a patrol of
Imperial Yeomanry near Doorn River Hut were shot on the
spot.

Report of Intelligence, East Cape Colony, July 29, 1901.—
Shooting of natives by Commandant Myburgh.

Report of Resident Magistrate, Aliwal North, July 30,
1901.—Shooting of natives at refugee camp.

August 23, 1901.—Native captured with a private of the
Black Watch near Clocolan and shot in his presence.

September 1, 1901.—Four natives with Colonel Dawkins's
column captured in Fauresmith district and shot by order of
Judge Hertzog.

Report of Resident Magistrate, Aliwal North, September 4,
1901.—Brutal treatment of natives by Boers under Bester,
J.P., of Aliwal North.

Report of Resident Magistrate, Riversdale, September 4,
1901.—Two coloured despatch riders severely flogged.

Report of Intelligence, South Cape Colony, September 18,
1901.—Natives murdered by Theron's orders.

Report of Chief Commissioner, Richmond, September 23, 1901.—Two unarmed natives shot by Commandant Malan.

Report of Resident Magistrate, Prieska, September 26, 1901.—Murder of two unarmed natives.

Report of Colonel Hickman, Ladismith, October 1, 1901.—Shooting of two natives by Scheepers.

Date uncertain.—A native in Petrusburg Gaol was shot in his cell by two Boers on the approach of the British troops.

So much for the Kaffir murders. It is to be earnestly hoped that no opportunism or desire to conciliate our enemies at the expense of justice will prevent a most thorough examination into every one of these black deeds, and a most stern punishment for the criminals.

I return, however, to the question of the conduct of the Boers to their white opponents. So long as they were fighting as an army under the eyes of the honourable men who led them, their conduct was on the whole good, but guerilla warfare brought with it the demoralisation which it always does bring, and there was a rapid falling away from the ordinary humanity between civilised opponents. I do not mean by this to assert that the Boer guerillas behaved as did the Spanish guerillas in 1810, or the Mexican in 1866. Such an assertion would be absurd. The Boers gave quarter and they received it. But several isolated instances, and several general cases have shown the demoralisation of their ranks. Of the former I might quote the circumstances of the death of Lieutenant Miers.

The official intimation was as follows:

'Pretoria: September 27.

'Lieutenant Miers, Somerset Light Infantry, employed with South African Constabulary, went out from his post at Riversdraai, 25th September, to meet three Boers approaching under white flag, who, after short conversation, were seen to shoot Lieutenant Miers dead and immediately gallop away. Inquiry being made and evidence recorded.'

A more detailed account was sent by the non-commissioned officer who was present. He described how the Boers approached the fort waving a white flag, how a corporal went out to them, and was told that they wished to speak with an officer, how Captain Miers rode out alone, and then:

'As soon as the officer had gone but a short distance on the far side of the spruit, the Boer with the white flag advanced to meet him; the officer also continued to advance till he came up with the blackguard. At the end of three or four minutes we saw the two walking back to the two Boers (who were standing a good two miles off from this fort of ours). When they reached the two Boers we saw the captain dismount, the group being barely visible owing to a rise in the ground. At the end of five or ten minutes we were just able to distinguish the sound of a shot, immediately after which we saw the officer's grey mare bolting westwards across the veldt riderless, with one of the Boers galloping for all he was worth after it.'

Of the general demoralisation here is the evidence of a witness in that very action at Graspan on June 6, which has been made so much of by the slanderers of our Army:

No. 4703 Lance-Corporal James Hanshaw, 2nd Batt. Bedfordshire Regiment, being duly sworn, states: 'At Graspan on June 6, 1901, I was present when we were attacked by the Boers, having previously captured a convoy from them. On going towards the wagons I found the Boers already there; finding we were outnumbered and resistance hopeless, we threw down our arms and held our hands up. Private Blunt, who was with me, shouted. "Don't shoot me, I have thrown down my rifle." The Boers then shot Private Blunt dead. He was holding his hands above his head at the time. Lieutenant Mair then shouted, "Have mercy, you cowards." The Boers then deliberately shot Lieutenant Mair dead as he was standing with his hands above his head. They then shot at Privates Pearse and Harvey, who were both standing with their hands up, the same bullet hitting Private Pearse in the nose, and killing Private Harvey. Two Boers then rushed from the wagons and threatened to shoot me, kicked me, and told me to lie down.'

No. 3253 Private E. Sewell, 2nd Batt. Bedfordshire Regiment, being duly sworn, states: 'I was at the fight at Graspan on June 6, 1901. About noon on that date the Boers attacked the convoy. I retired to Lieutenant Mair's party, when, finding we were outnumbered and surrounded, we put our hands up. The Boers took our arms from us and retired round some kraals; shortly afterwards they came back, and two men shouted, "Hands up." We said we were already prisoners, and that our arms had been collected. Private Blunt held up his hands, and at the same time said, "Don't shoot me, I am already hands up." The Boers then said, "Take that," and shot him through the stomach. Lieutenant Mair then stepped out from the wagons, and said, "Have mercy, you cowards." The Boer then shot him dead from his horse. The Boer was sitting on his horse almost touching Lieutenant Mair at the time. The Boer then shot at Lance-Corporal Harvey and Private Pearse, who were standing together with their hands up above their heads, the shot wounding Private Pearse and killing Lance-Corporal Harvey.'

Here is the evidence of the murder of the wounded at Vlakfontein on May 29, 1901:

Private D. Chambers, H Company, 1st Batt. Derbyshire Regiment, being duly sworn, states: 'Whilst lying on the ground wounded I saw a Boer shoot two of our wounded who were lying on the ground near me. This Boer also fired at me, but missed me.'

Privates W. Bacon and Charles Girling, 1st Batt. Derbyshire Regiment, being duly sworn, state: 'Whilst lying wounded on the ground with two other wounded men four Boers came up to us, dismounted, and fired a volley at us. We were all hit again, and Private Goodwin, of our regiment, was killed. The Boers then took our arms away, and after swearing at us rode away.'

Corporal Sargent, 1st Batt. Derbyshire Regiment, being duly sworn, states: 'While lying wounded behind a rock I saw a Boer shoot a Yeomanry officer who was walking away, wounded in the hand.'

Acting-Sergeant Chambers, 69th Company Imperial Yeomanry, being duly sworn, states: 'I saw a Boer, a short man with a dark beard, going round carrying his rifle under his arm, as one would carry a sporting rifle, and shoot three of our wounded.'

Private A. C. Bell, 69th Company Imperial Yeomanry, being duly sworn, states: 'I heard a Boer call to one of our men to put up his hands, and when he did so the Boer shot him from about fifteen yards off; I was about twenty yards off.'

Private T. George, 69th Company Imperial Yeomanry, being duly sworn, states: 'I was walking back to camp wounded, when I saw a Boer about seventeen years of age shoot at a wounded Derby man who was calling for water; the Boer then came up to me and took my bandolier away.'

Gunner W. H. Blackburn, 28th Battery Royal Field Artillery, being duly sworn, states: 'I saw a Boer take a rifle and bandolier from a wounded Derby man, and then shoot him; the Boer then came to me and asked me for my rifle; I showed it him where it was lying on the ground.'

Things of this sort are progressive. Here is what occurred at Brakenlaagte when the rear of Benson's column was destroyed.

Major N. E. Young, D.S.O., Royal Field Artillery, sends the report to the Commander-in-Chief of Boer cruelty to the officers and men wounded in the action with Colonel Benson's column at Brakenlaagte. It is dated Pretoria, November 7, and Lord Kitchener's covering letter is dated November 9.

Major Young, who made the inquiries into the charges of cruelty in accordance with Lord Kitchener's instructions, says:

'Out of a total of 147 wounded non-commissioned officers and men seen by me fifty-four had not been in the hands of the Boers. Of the remaining ninety-three men, eighteen informed me they had nothing to complain of.

'Seventy-five non-commissioned officers and men made complaint of ill- treatment of a more or less serious nature; nearly all of these had been robbed of whatever money they possessed, also of their watches and private papers.

'Many had been deprived of other articles of clothing, hats, jackets, and socks, in some cases being left with an old shirt and a pair of drawers only.

'There is a consensus of opinion that the wounded lying round the guns were fired on by Boers, who had already disarmed them, for a long period, after all firing in their neighbourhood from our side had ceased.

'Even the late Colonel Benson was not respected, though he was protected for some time by a man in authority; eventually his spurs, gaiters, and private papers were removed.'

Major Young, in concluding his report, says:—

'I was impressed with the idea that the statements made to me were true and not wilfully exaggerated, so simply were they made. There seems no doubt that though the Boer commandants have the will they have no longer the power to repress outrage and murder on the part of their subordinates.'

Lieutenant G. Acland Troyte, King's Royal Rifle Corps, 25th Mounted Infantry, states: 'I was wounded on October 25 in a rearguard action with Colonel Benson's force, near Kaffirstadt. The Boers came up and stripped me of everything except my drawers, shirt, and socks, they gave me an old pair of trousers, and later a coat.'

Lieutenant Reginald Seymour, 1st Batt. King's Royal Rifle Corps, 25th Mounted Infantry:—'On October 30 my company was sent back to the support of Colonel Benson's rearguard. I was wounded early in the day. The Boers came up. They took my greatcoat, gaiters, spurs, and helmet; they took the money and watches from the other wounded, but left them their clothes except the coat of one man. They then left us without assistance. Two Boers afterwards returned and took away a greatcoat belonging to one of our men which had been left over me. One of the party who stripped us was addressed by the remainder as Commandant.'

Captain C. W. Collins, Cheshire Regiment:—'I was signalling officer to Colonel Benson on October 30. I was wounded, and lying near the guns about a hundred yards in rear of them. A field-cornet came up and went away without molesting me. At about 5.30 P.M., or a little later, the ambulances came and picked me up; my ambulance went on some distance farther, and Colonel Benson and some men were put in it. There seemed to be a lot of delay, which annoyed the Colonel, and he asked to be allowed to get away. The delay, however, continued till a Boer came and took away Colonel Benson's documents from his pocket, notwithstanding his protest that they were all private papers, and that they had been seen by a commandant earlier in the day, who said they were not required.'

Private E. Rigby, 4th Batt. King's Royal Rifle Corps, states the Boers took all his clothes except his shirt. This man is not quite able to speak yet.

Trooper Hood, 2nd Scottish Horse: 'While I was lying wounded on the ground the Boers came up and stripped me of my hat and coat, boots, 15s., and a metal watch. I saw them fire at another wounded man as he was coming to me for a drink.'

Trooper Alexander Main, 2nd Scottish Horse: 'While lying on the ground, the Boers came close up and stood about fifteen to twenty yards away from where we were lying wounded round the guns. All were wounded at this time, and no one was firing. I saw the Boers there fire at the wounded. Captain Lloyd, a staff officer, was lying beside me wounded in the leg at this time; he received one or two more shots in the body, and shortly afterwards he died. I myself received three more wounds.'

Trooper Jamieson, Scottish Horse: 'The Boers took off his boots and they hurt his shattered arm in a terrible manner while getting off his bandolier. His arm has been removed.'

Private Parrish, 1st Batt. King's Royal Rifle Corps: 'Our ridge was not firing any more, but whenever a wounded man showed himself, they fired at him, in this way several were killed; one man who was waving a bit of blue stuff with the idea of getting an ambulance, received about twenty shots.'

Private Prickett, 4th Batt. King's Royal Rifle Corps: 'On October 30 I was lying wounded. I saw the Boers come up, and an old Boer with black beard and whiskers, and wearing leggings, whom I should be able to recognise again, shot my friend, Private F. Foster, 4th Batt. King's Royal Rifle Corps, by putting the muzzle of his rifle to his side. Private Foster had been firing under cover of an ant-heap till the Boers took the position; he then threw away his rifle to put his hands up, but was shot all the same.'

Private N. H. Grierson, Scottish Horse: 'I was wounded and lying by the side of Colonel Benson. When the Boers came up they wanted to begin to loot; Colonel Benson stopped them, telling them he had received a letter from Commandant Grobelaar saying the wounded would be respected. Colonel Benson asked if he could see Grobelaar; they said they would fetch him, and brought up someone who was in authority, but I do not think it was Grobelaar. Colonel Benson told him the wounded were not to be touched, and he said he would do his best; he himself protected Colonel Benson for about an hour, but he was still there when a Boer took off Colonel Benson's spurs and gaiters.'

Sergeant Ketley, 7th Hussars: 'I was wounded in the head and hip just before the Boers rushed the guns. I was covered with blood. A Boer came up, took away my carbine and revolver and asked me to put up my hands. I could not do this, being too weak with the loss of blood. He loaded my own carbine and aimed from his breast while kneeling, and pointed at my breast. He fired and hit me in the right arm just below the shoulder.'

Private Bell, 4th Batt. King's Royal Rifle Corps, 25th Mounted Infantry: 'When the Boers came up they took my boots off very roughly, hurting my wounded leg very much. I saw them taking watches and money off the other men.'

Private C. Connor, Royal Dublin Fusiliers: 'I was lying beside the guns among a lot of our wounded, who were not firing. Every time one of our wounded attempted to move the Boers fired at them; several men (about ten or eleven) were killed in this way.'

Lieutenant Bircham, 4th Batt. King's Royal Rifle Corps: 'Was in the same ambulance wagon as Lieutenant Martin, King's Own Yorkshire Light Infantry (since deceased), and the latter told him that when he (Lieutenant Martin) was lying on the ground wounded the Boers took off his spurs and gaiters. In taking off his spurs they wrenched his leg, the bone of which was shattered, completely round, so as to be able to get at the spurs more easily, though Lieutenant Martin told them where he was hit.'

Corporal P. Gower, 4th Batt. King's Royal Rifle Corps, 25th Mounted Infantry: 'I was wounded and unconscious. When I came to, the Boers were stripping the men round me. A man, Private Foster, who was not five yards from me, put up his hands in token of surrender, but was shot at about five-yards range by a tall man with a black beard. He was killed.'

Corporal Atkins, 84th Battery Royal Field Artillery: 'The Boers came up to me and said, "Can you work this gun?" I said, "Yes." He said, "Get up and show me." I said, "How can I? I have one hand taken away, and I am wounded in both legs"—this last was not true. He then said, "Give us your boots"—he took them and my mackintosh. He took what money was in my belt. One of our men, Bombardier Collins, got up to try and put up a white flag, as we were being fired at both from the camp and by the Boers; as soon as he got up they began shooting at him. I saw a Kaffir fire three shots from about thirty yards off.'

Bombardier Collins, 84th Battery Royal Field Artillery: 'When lying wounded near the guns after the Boers had been up to them I tried to raise a white flag as our own people were dropping their bullets close to us. When I did this they fired at me.'

So long as an excuse could be found for a brave enemy we found it. But the day is rapidly approaching when we must turn to the world with our evidence and say, 'Are these the deeds of soldiers or of brigands? If they act as brigands, then, why must we forever treat them as soldiers?' I have read letters from soldiers who saw their own comrades ill-treated at Brakenlaagte. I trust that they will hold their hands, but it is almost more than can be asked of human nature.

XI. CONCLUSIONS

I have now dealt with the various vexed questions of the war, and have, I hope, said enough to show that we have no reason to blush for our soldiers, but only for those of their fellow-countrymen who have traduced them. But there are a number of opponents of the war who have never descended to such baseness, and who honestly hold that the war might have been avoided, and also that we might, after it broke out, have found some terms which the Boers could accept. At their back they have all those amiable and goodhearted idealists who have not examined the question very critically, but are oppressed by the fear that the Empire is acting too roughly towards these pastoral republics. Such an opinion is just as honest as, and infinitely more respectable than, that of some journalists whose arrogance at the beginning of the war brought shame upon us. There is no better representative of such views than Mr. Methuen in his 'Peace or War,' an able and moderate statement. Let us examine his conclusions, omitting the causes of the war, which have already been treated at some length.

Mr. Methuen draws a close comparison between the situation and that of the American Revolution. There are certainly points of resemblance—and also of difference. Our cause was essentially unjust with the Americans and essentially just with the Boers. We have the Empire at our back now. We have the command of the seas. We are very wealthy. These are all new and important factors.

The revolt of the Boer States against the British suzerainty is much more like the revolt of the Southern States against the Government of Washington. The situation here after Colenso was that of the North after Bull's Run. Mr. Methuen has much to say of Boer bitterness, but was it greater than Southern bitterness? That war was fought to a finish and we see what has come of it. I do not claim that the parallel is exact, but it is at least as nearly exact as that from which Mr. Methuen draws such depressing conclusions. He has many gloomy remarks upon our prospects, but it is in facing gloomy prospects with a high heart that a nation proves that it is not yet degenerate. Better pay all the price which he predicts than shrink for one instant from our task.

Mr. Methuen makes a good deal of the foolish and unchivalrous, even brutal, way in which some individuals and some newspapers have spoken of the enemy. I suppose there are few gentlemen who have not winced at such remarks. But let Mr. Methuen glance at the continental press and see the work of the supporters of the enemy. It will make him feel more charitable towards his boorish fellow-countrymen. Or let him examine the Dutch press in South Africa and see if all the abuse is on one side. Here are some appreciations from the first letter of P.S. (of Colesburg) in the 'Times':

'Your lazy, dirty, drunken, lower classes.'

'Your officers are pedantic scholars or frivolous society men.'

'The major part of your population consists of females, cripples, epileptics, consumptives, cancerous people, invalids, and lunatics of all kinds.'

'Nine-tenths of your statesmen and higher officials are suffering from kidney disease.'

'We will not be governed by a set of British curs.'

No great chivalry or consideration of the feelings of one's opponent there! Here is a poem from the 'Volksstem' on August 26, 1899, weeks before the war, describing the Boer programme. A translation runs thus:

> 'Then shall our ears with pleasure listen
> To widow's wail and orphan's cry;
> And shall we gird, as joyful witness,
> The death-watch of your villainy.
>
> 'Then shall we massacre and butcher
> You, and swallow glad your blood;

And count it "capital with interest"—
Villain's interest—sweet and good.

'And when the sun shall set in Heaven,
Dark with the clouds of steaming blood,
A ghastly, woeful, dying murmur
Will be the Briton's last salute.

'Then shall we start our jolly banquet,
And toast the first "the British blood."'

No doubt a decent Boer would be as ashamed of this as we are of some of our Jingo papers. But even their leaders, Reitz, Steyn, and Kruger, have allowed themselves to use language about the British which cannot, fortunately, be matched upon our side.

Mr. Methuen is severe upon Lord Salisbury for the uncompromising nature of his reply to the Presidents' overtures for peace in March 1900. But what other practical course could he suggest? Is it not evident that if independence were left to the Boers the war would have been without result, since all the causes which led to it would be still open and unsolved. On the morrow of such a peace we should be faced by the Franchise question, the Uitlander question, and every other question for the settling of which we have made such sacrifices. Is that a sane policy? Is it even tenable on the grounds of humanity, since it is perfectly clear that it must lead to another and a greater struggle in the course of a few years? When the work was more than half done it would have been madness to hold our hand.

Surely there is no need for gloomy forebodings. The war has seemed long to us who have endured it, but to our descendants it will probably seem a very short time for the conquest of so huge a country and so stubborn a foe. Our task is not endless. Four-fifths of the manhood of the country is already in our hands, and the fifth remaining diminishes week by week. Our mobility and efficiency increase. There is not the slightest ground for Mr. Methuen's lament about the condition of the Army. It is far fitter than when it began. It is mathematically certain that a very few months must see the last commando hunted down. Meanwhile civil life is gaining strength once more. Already the Orange River Colony pays its own way, and the Transvaal is within measurable distance of doing the same. Industries are waking up, and on the Rand the roar of the stamps has replaced that of the cannon. Fifteen hundred of them will soon be at work, and the refugees are returning at the rate of 400 a week.

It is argued that the bitterness of this struggle will never die out, but history has shown that it is the fights which are fought to an absolute finish which leave the least rancour. Remember Lee's noble words: 'We are a Christian people. We have fought this fight as long and as well as we knew how. We have been defeated. For us, as a Christian people, there is now but one course to pursue. We must accept the situation.' That is how a brave man accepts the judgment of the God of battles. So it may at last be with the Boers. These prison camps and concentration camps have at least brought them, men and women, in contact with our people. Perhaps the memories left behind will not be entirely bitter. Providence works in strange ways, and possibly the seeds of reconciliation, may be planted even there.

As to the immediate future it is probable that the Transvaal, with the rush of immigrants which prosperity will bring, will soon be, next to Natal, the most British of the South African States. With Natal British, Rhodesia British, the Transvaal British, the Cape half and half, and only the Orange River Colony Dutch, the British would be assured of a majority in a parliament of United South Africa. It would be well to allow Natal to absorb the Vryheid district of the Transvaal.

It has occurred to me—a suggestion which I put forward with all diffidence—that it would be a wise and practicable step to form a Boer Reservation in the northern districts of the Transvaal (Watersberg and Zoutpansberg). Let them live there as Basutos live in Basutoland, or Indians in Indian territory, or the inhabitants of a protected state in India. Guarantee them, as long as they remain peaceable under the British flag, complete protection from the invasion of the miner or the prospector. Let them live their own lives in their own way, with some simple form of home rule of their own. The irreconcilable men who could never rub shoulders with the British could find a home there, and the British colonies would be all the stronger for the placing in quarantine of those who might infect their neighbours with their own bitterness. Such a State could not be a serious source of danger, since we could control all the avenues by which arms could reach it. I am aware that the Watersberg and the Zoutpansberg are not very desirable places of residence, but the thing is voluntary and no man would need to go there unless he wished. Without some such plan the Empire will have no safety-valve in South Africa.

I cannot conclude this short review of the South African question without some allusion to the attitude of continental nations during the struggle. This has been in all cases correct upon the part of the governments, and in nearly all cases incorrect upon the part of the people. A few brave and clear-headed men, like Yves Guyot in France, and M. Tallichet and M. Naville in Switzerland, have been our friends, or rather the friends of truth; but the vast majority of all nations have been carried away by that flood of prejudice and lies which has had its source in a venal, or at best an ignorant, press. In this country the people in the long run can always impose its will upon the Government, and it has, I believe, come to some very definite conclusions which will affect British foreign policy for many years to come.

Against France there is no great bitterness, for we feel that France has never had much reason to look upon us in any light save that of an enemy. For many years we have wished to be friendly, but the traditions of centuries are not so easily forgotten. Besides, some of our shortcomings are of recent date. Many of us were, and are, ashamed of the absurd and hysterical outcry in this country over the Dreyfus case. Are there no miscarriages of justice in the Empire? An expression of opinion was permissible, but the wholesale national abuse has disarmed us from resenting some equally immoderate criticism of our own character and morals. To Russia also we can bear no grudge, for we know that there is no real public opinion in that country, and that their press has no means for forming first-hand conclusions. Besides, in this case also there is a certain secular enmity which may account for a warped judgment.

But it is very different with Germany. Again and again in the world's history we have been the friends and the allies of these people. It was so in the days of Marlborough, in those of the Great Frederick, and in those of Napoleon. When we could not help them with men we helped them with money. Our fleet has crushed their enemies. And now, for the first time in history, we have had a chance of seeing who were our friends in Europe, and nowhere have we met more hatred and more slander than from the German press and the German people. Their most respectable journals have not hesitated to represent the British troops—troops every bit as humane and as highly disciplined as their own—not only as committing outrages on person and property, but even as murdering women and children.

At first this unexpected phenomenon merely surprised the British people, then it pained them, and, finally, after two years of it, it has roused a deep and enduring anger in their minds. There is a rumour which crops up from time to time, and which appears to have some foundation, that there is a secret agreement by which the Triple Alliance can, under certain circumstances, claim the use of the British fleet. There are, probably, only a few men in Europe who know whether this is so or not. But if it is, it would be only fair to denounce such a treaty as soon as may be, for very many years must pass before it would be possible for the public to forget and forgive the action of Germany. Nor can we entirely exonerate the German Government, for we know the Germans to be a well-disciplined people; and we cannot believe that Anglophobia could have reached the point of mania without some official encouragement—or, at least, in the face of any official discouragement.

The agitation reached its climax in the uproar over the reference which Mr. Chamberlain made to the war of 1870 in his speech at Edinburgh. In this speech Mr. Chamberlain very justly remarked that we could find precedents for any severe measures which we might be compelled to take against the guerillas, in the history of previous campaigns— those of the French in Algiers, the Russians in the Caucasus, the Austrians in Bosnia, and the Germans in France. Such a remark implied, of course, no blame upon these respective countries, but pointed out the martial precedents which justify such measures. It is true that the Germans in France never found any reason to lay the country waste, for they were never faced with a universal guerilla warfare as we have been, but they gave the *franc-tireur*, or the man who was found cutting the wire of the line, very short shrift;

whereas we have never put to death a single *bonâ-fide*Boer for this offence. Possibly it was not that the Germans were too severe, but that we were too lax. In any case, it is evident that there was nothing offensive in the statement, and those who have been well informed as to the doings of the British soldiers in the war will know that any troops in the world might be proud to be classed with them, either in valour or humanity.

But the agitators did not even trouble to ascertain the words which Mr. Chamberlain had used—though they might have seen them in the original on the table of the *Lesezimmer* of the nearest hotel. On the strength of a garbled report a tumult arose over the whole country and many indignation meetings were held. Six hundred and eighty clergymen were found whose hearts and heads were soft enough to be imposed upon by absurd tales of British atrocities, and these reverend gentlemen subscribed an insulting protest against them. The whole movement was so obviously artificial—or at least based upon misapprehension—that it excited as much amusement as anger in this country; but still the honour of our Army is very dear to us, and the continued attacks upon it have left an enduring feeling of resentment amongst us, which will not, and should not, die away in this generation. It is not too much to say that five years ago a complete defeat by Germany in a European war would have certainly caused British intervention. Public sentiment and racial affinity would never have allowed us to see her really go to the wall. And now it is certain that in our lifetime no British guinea and no soldier's life would under any circumstances be spent for such an end. That is one strange result of the Boer war, and in the long run it is possible that it may prove not the least important.

Yet some allowance must be made for people who for years have had only one side of the question laid before them, and have had that one side supported by every sort of malignant invention and misrepresentation. Surely the day will come when truth will prevail, if only for the reason that the sources of corruption will run dry. It is difficult to imagine that any permanent policy can ever be upheld by falsehood. When that day does come, and the nations of Europe see how they have been hoodwinked and made tools of by a few artful and unscrupulous men, it is possible that a tardy justice will be done to the dignity and inflexible resolution which Great Britain has shown throughout. Until the dawn breaks we can but go upon our way, looking neither to the right nor to the left, but keeping our eyes fixed ever upon one great object—a South Africa in which there shall never again be strife, and in which Boer and Briton shall enjoy the same rights and the same liberties, with a common law to shield them and a common love of their own fatherland to weld them into one united nation.

Arthur Conan Doyle – A Short Biography

The Scottish physician and writer Sir Arthur Ignatius Conan Doyle's name is inseparable from the phenomenon of Sherlock Holmes, undoubtedly his greatest character and the eponymous meticulous, deductive and frankly genius hero of crime fiction. However, his prolific writing was in more than just the crime fiction genre; alongside the 56 short stories and 4 novels of Sherlock Holmes he explored science fiction and fantasy as well as plays, historical novels and poetry. Another of Conan Doyle's notable characters is Professor Challenger, whose aggression and dominance serves as the antithesis of Holmes, and demonstrates Conan Doyle's capacious imagination and dramatic skill. Returning to his name, it is worthy of note that there is uncertainty surrounding his surname; while he is often referred to as Conan Doyle, where Conan and Doyle are treated as a compound surname, the entry at his baptism records Arthur Ignatius Conan as first names, and Doyle as a solitary last. Indeed, his father's name was simply Doyle. Moreover, the catalogues of the British Library and the Library of Congress insist of Doyle as his surname. Regardless, he began to refer to himself as Conan Doyle and his second wife would take this as her surname, so he will herein be referred to as Conan Doyle, in accordance with his apparent preference.

He was born in Edinburgh at 11 Picardy Place on 22nd May 1859 to his parents Charles Altamont Doyle, an Englishman of Irish descent, and Mary (née Foley), an Irishwoman, who had married in 1855. He had a brother named Innes. Charles was developing an alcohol dependence which would become incompatible with family life, and they dispersed in 1864 at which point the children were temporarily housed at various addresses across Edinburgh. They reunited in 1867, only to live together at 3 Sciennes place in a squalid tenement flat. Fortunately for the children, they had wealthy uncles who were willing to support them by paying for education and clothing. Accordingly at the age of nine Conan Doyle was sent to Hodder Place, Stonyhurst, a Roman Catholic Jesuit preparatory school. He was here for the two years between 1868 and 1870 at which point he went on to Stonyhurst College where he stayed until 1875 when he went for a year to Stella Matutina, Jesuit school in Feldkirch, Austria.

This school education set him up for a place at the University of Edinburgh, where he studied medicine between 1876 and 1881. Part of his course involved placements in Aston, (now a suburb of Birmingham, though at the time it was its own town), Sheffield and in Ruyton-XI-Towns, an unusually named village in Shropshire which acquired its numeral when, in the twelfth century, a castle was built there which became the focus of eleven small and disparate communities. It was during this study that he began writing short stories, with the successful submission of 'The Haunted Grange of Goresthorpe' to Blackwood's Magazine arguably his greatest literary achievement at the time. As well as this recognition, he saw his first published piece 'The Mystery of the Sasassa Valley', a story set in South Africa, printed on 6th September 1879 in Chambers's Edinburgh Journal, and only 17 days later his first non-fiction article was published in the British Medical Journal on 20th September, entitled 'Gelsemium as poison'. Having finished his studies he took an appointment as a Doctor on the Greenland whaler Hope of Peterhead in 1880 and then, following his graduation, he assumed the role of ship's surgeon on the SS Mayumba during its 1881 voyage to the West African coast.

1882 saw his move to Plymouth where he joined the medical practice of former classmate George Turnavine Budd, though they had a difficult professional relationship and Conan Doyle left shortly thereafter in order to set up his own independent practice. Having arrived in Portsmouth in June of that year and disembarked the SS Mayumba with a mere £10 (£700 today) to his name, he proceeded to establish his practice at 1 Bush Billas in Elm Grove, Southsea, a seaside town in the country of Hampshire. He was not met with initial success, and in order to pass the time between visits from patients he resumed his story writing. During this period he completed his first novel, The Mystery of Cloomber, though it was not published until 1888, and the unfinished Narrative of John Smith, which only recently saw publication in 2011. Alongside these longer works was the steady production of a portfolio of short stories which included 'The Captain of the Pole-Star' and 'J. Habakuk Jephson's Statement', both inspired by the time he spent at sea. Meanwhile, in 1885 he completed a doctorate on the subject of tabes dorsalis, the slow degradation and demyelination of the sensory neurons that carry afferent information. He also married Louisa Hawkins, who was the sister of one of his patients, that same year. However, two years after this marriage he met and fell in love with Jean Elizabeth Leckie, though he maintained a platonic relationship with her out of respect for and loyalty to his wife for whom he still had great affection.

Though he struggled to find a publisher for the stories he wrote in these stretches of inactivity, his literary career would take an historic turn in 1886 when, on 20th November, Ward Lock & Co offered Conan Doyle £25 for all rights to A Study In Scarlet. The first and one of the most famous of the Sherlock Holmes franchise, it introduced the public to a new, empirical and methodical mode of crime fiction, and indeed criminality itself, by the combination of a perspicacious, brilliantly observant and data-driven detective whose army doctor companion Watson provided further scientific support as well as a means of observing and narrating Holmes's processes and adventures. The novel was a success; a letter from Robert Louis Stevenson who had acquired a copy of the novel in Samoa, wrote with "his compliments on your very ingenious very interesting adventures of Sherlock Holmes", while noting the similarity between Holmes's methods and a certain Joseph Bell, upon whom Holmes was based. Conan Doyle even wrote to Bell explaining so, and that "round the centre of deduction and inference and observation which I have heard you inculcate I have tried to build up a man". It was met with positive reviews in The Scotsman and The Herald and this success encouraged Ward Lock & Co to commission a sequel, The Sign of Four, which appeared in Lippincott's Magazine in February 1890, under agreement with the Ward Lock company. On 28th January 1889 his first child was born,

Mary Louise, and three years later on 15th November 1892 they had a boy, Arthur Alleyne Kingsley, who became known only as Kingsley.

Now that he had a family to look after, he began to look more closely at the arrangement he had with his publishers and Conan Doyle soon began to feel that, as a new, inexperienced writer, he had been somewhat exploited by them, resolving to curtail his involvement with their business and instead beginning to write for the Strand Magazine from his home at 2 Wimpole Street. Meanwhile Conan Doyle was enjoying something of a sporting career, playing under the pseudonym A.C. Smith as goalkeeper for Portsmouth Association Football Club (though this club had no connection to present-day Portsmouth F.C, founded two years after Conan Doyle's amateur side disbanded in 1896). He was also a keen cricketer and played ten first-class matches between 1899 and 1907 for the Marylebone Cricket Club, making a highest score with the bat of 43 against London County. As an occasional bowler he only took one wicket in these ten matches, though it was W.G. Grace's stumps which he hit; a notable triumph of the right arm. His sporting interests extended to golf, for which he was elected captain of the Crowborough Beacon Golf Club in East Sussex for 1910. He once even visited Rudyard Kipling at his farm in America, bringing with him a set of golf clubs and giving his fellow famous writer an extended two-day lesson.

He went to Vienna to study ophthalmology in 1890 before returning to London and setting up a practice as an ophthalmologist, though he recorded in his autobiography that not a single patient ever crossed his doorway. This left him with more time for his writing, though by now he was beginning to feel somewhat exhausted by Holmes and wrote to his mother in 1891 "I think of slaying Holmes ... and winding him up for good and all. He takes my mind from better things." This was met with an entreaty from his mother of "you won't! You can't! You mustn't!" These "better things" were his historical novels such as The White Company (1891) and The Great Shadow (1892). Then, in defiance of his mother and the wishes of the general public, in December 1893 he wrote Holmes's apparent death in the clutches of a high-consequence brawl with arch-nemesis Moriarty above the Reichenbach Falls in Germany. Both of their deaths seemed certain, and it seemed the end of the Sherlock Holmes phenomenon. He now had time to focus on other work, most notably his pamphlet justifying the United Kingdom's involvement with the Boer War, an involvement for which they were frequently and heavily criticised. The War in South Africa: Its Cause and Conduct was widely translated after its publication in 1902, and was based to a certain extent on the time he had spent as a volunteer doctor in the Langman Field Hospital at Bloemfontein between March and June 1900. It was this and his book The Great Boer War, written in 1900, which he considered the reasons for his knighthood in 1902 by King Edward VII, and he was subsequently appointed Deputy-Lieutenant of Surrey. In 1903 however, owing to the public demand of which he became increasingly aware after successive letters from fans pleading for the resurrection of their great hero, he seemingly brought Holmes back from the dead; in 'The Adventure of the Empty House', the first story for ten years, he reassures the reader that Holmes had merely arranged for his fall to appear fatal in order that his other enemies (particularly Colonel Sebastian Moran) might consider him dead also, whereas in reality he never falls at all. Fans were ecstatic and Conan Doyle continued to write Holmes stories.

His interest in politics piqued by the issues surrounding the Boer War, the interest he had in criminal justice which was so prominent in his crime fiction transferred to that of real-life and he became a fervent advocate of justice, investigating two closed cases of incorrect conviction. The first, in 1906, saw the shy half-British, half-Indian lawyer George Edalji exonerated for imprisonment for crimes of mutilation towards animals which he hadn't committed. Though the police were convinced of their prosecution, the crimes continued even after he was imprisoned and Conan Doyle, analytical and methodical as his invention, proceeded to privately investigate the case and the outcome, Edalji's acquittal, encouraged the establishment of the Court of Criminal Appeal in 1907. Meanwhile his wife Louisa had been suffering from tuberculosis and died on the 4th July, and Conan Doyle married Jean Elizabeth Leckie, the woman with whom he had fallen in love in 1897, the year after. The second case of injustice was some twenty years later, though pertaining to a crime committed in 1908 allegedly by one Oscar Slater, a German Jew and gambling-den operator convicted of bludgeoning an 82 year old woman to death. Conan Doyle noticed inconsistencies in the evidence which, combined with his general sense of unease about the case, motivated him to pay for the majority of Slater's legal fees and eventually see him released in 1928.

He now had his first child with Jean, whom they named Denis Percy Stewart and was born on 17th March 1909, and then on 19th November 1910 they had Adrian Malcolm. Jean Lena Annette followed on 21st December 1912. Over the next few years there would be various deaths in his family. His first wife having already passed away, Kingsley was taken ill after complications of pneumonia following injury near the Somme in 1917. His two brothers-in-law also died, and after Kingsley's condition worsened and he passed away on 28th October owing to the complications of his convalescence and his brother Innes, now Brigadier-General died of the same, Conan Doyle sank into a deep depression, eventually finding solace in Christian spiritualism. Despite the veracity of his writing, he was not free from misunderstanding. Convinced of the authenticity of five (now known to be) hoaxed photographs of fairies by Elsie Wright in June 1917, he wrote a book The Coming of the Fairies in 1921 exploring them and other supernatural phenomena, followed up in 1926 by The History of Spiritualism, a broader look at the particulars of the movement. Encouraging the Spiritualists' National Union to modify their precepts, his turn to spiritualism was so strong that he wrote a Professor Challenger novel on the subject, entitled The Land of Mist, in 1926.

His friendship with Harry Houdini, another noted Spiritualist, led him to believe that Houdini was possessed of supernatural powers and that his feats were not tricks but proof of the supernatural. He expresses this view in The Edge of the Unknown (1930), and Houdini's inability to convince Conan Doyle of the illusory nature of his feats led to a bitter and very public falling-out. Conan Doyle has been posthumously implicated in the Piltdown Man hoax (and even accused of being its perpetrator by Richard Milner), a discovery of fossilised hominid remains which fooled the scientific world for over 40 years. Milner posits that Conan Doyle's motive was revenge on the scientific establishment for their debunking of Houdini, and that within The Lost World which was released the year the remains were found contains several hidden and encrypted clues indicating his involvement.

But for a moment let us refer back to Arthur Conan Doyle the historian. In essence he is simply under rated or unfortunately ignored. Certainly the high standard and popularity of his other works overshadows this facet of his writing. Among his works of politics and the military are found the well known volumes on the Boer war and the

South African war. Additionally he wrote a much admired pamphlet on the coming First world War based on refuting the work by a German General. It proved prophetic in the end; the Nations did engage in a colossal war with various allies at their sides that wreaked havoc on an entire generation and sowed the seeds for an even greater calamity. Doyle was to write 6 volumes tracking the war and they remain an invaluable guide as they were written during and shortly after the war.

On 7th July 1930 Conan Doyle was discovered in the hall of Windlesham Manor, his house in Crowborough, East Sussex, clutching his chest. He died of a heart attack at the age of 71, and his last words, directed to his wife, were "you are wonderful". As a Spiritualist, his burial brought controversy as there was debate as to where he should properly be buried. Eventually he was interred on 11th July in Windlesham rose garden, though he was later removed and buried with his wife in Minstead churchyard in the New Forest, Hampshire. The epitaph on that gravestone reads

Steel true
Blade straight
Arthur Conan Doyle
Knight
Patriot, Physician and man of letters

www.ingramcontent.com/pod-product-compliance
Lightning Source LLC
Chambersburg PA
CBHW061432040426
42450CB00007B/1009